MW01223346

Out of Line

Fiction, Poetry, Essays

THEMES OF

PEACE AND JUSTICE

EDITED BY

SAM LONGMIRE

GARDEN HOUSE PRESS

www.gardenhousepress.net

ACKNOWLEDGMENT

Baila Litton has provided the following commentary about her works that appear on the front and back cover, Herstories #3 and Herstories #1, 60"x40", M.M. on rice paper.

"Each person we encounter is a unique mapping of qualities and energies that are invisible to the naked eye. Often, we seem to react to each other based on skin-to-skin appraisals or other superficialities. Yet, some part of us intuits the presence of much, much more.

Herstories are an ongoing series of mixed media paintings exploring the face as a mask and the tattoo as the indelible mark, shield, and sacrifice. This body of work is layered with many skins of collaged paper, drawings, paint, and bits of fabric. The skins transform the mask into the portrait and bring surface and depth together as one. The markings include ancient characters, symbols, and maps."

Baila Litton has been featured in numerous group and solo exhibitions nationally, including Huntington Museum of Art in Huntington, West Virginia; The University Art Gallery, Indiana State University; The McDonough Museum of Art, and The Massillon Museum, among others. She had a solo exhibition of her work at The Butler Institute of American Art in Youngstown, Ohio, and in 2004-2005 had solo exhibitions in Buenos Aires, Argentina, and Dayton, Ohio. Her work was featured in New American Paintings Vol.#23. Baila Litton is a recipient of The Ohio Arts Council Individual Artist Fellowship in 2000 and 2003. Her work is included in many private and corporate collections. She currently resides in Cleveland, Ohio.

Out of Line

Table of Contents

Out of Line

TABLE OF CONTENTS

Part III   Dissonance

I

AFTER WAR BEGINS

On the Morning After War Begins
Louise A. Blum

You watch now – people are going to get quiet
Even ones who used to talk
now and then
furtively
looking over their shoulders

People are going to freeze
fall into step
lockstep
support our troops
as if advocating for peace
does not support them

You watch –
War kills, maims, distorts
and here at home
it slips its hands around our throats
and steals our voice
the second we hold our tongues

War Torn

Carol Alena Aronoff

Fourteen children
flew away
this morning.
They left behind
memories
of shattered glass,
took only a wisp
of blanket
or ragged doll,
pleading
for sunrise
to light their way.

It was their last request.

Return to Peace

Carol Alena Aronoff

When did peace become passé,
consigned to collective memory
banks like old currency?
Tattered flags, faded tee shirts,
the last remnants
of a once noble cause.

It used to be a virtue—
like love, like *you're my brother.*
Embroidered on jeans, its symbol
hung in windows—the blood of lambs
on Passover doors.

We exalted those who sought it,
awarded the Nobel prize, greeted
opponents with raised fingers—
for nonviolent victory—peace
streaming out an open hand.

Now it has gone the way of liberals,
free speech movements, Bill of Rights.
Where once war was thought to be
obsolete, we have preemptive
battles, surgical strikes.

What happened to a *kinder, gentler
nation, the thousand points of light?*
Without the balm of peace,
the medicine of equality,
there is no cure for terror.

The Sacrifice

Carol Alena Aronoff

He was just a boy;
his voice still cracked, growth
plates not yet closed— eyes,
bewildered, boring holes
in our global conscience.

Explosives strapped around
his waist were not his own;
the too large shoes once lived
with an older, richer Arab boy.

The words, someone else's,
bespoke their desperate origin;
he couldn't swallow them whole,
didn't want to die for some far-off,
maybe paradise, who knows?

We grew a little that day—seeing
children sent to fight our wars,
to die, childhoods swept away
at birth by pious dogmas.

What gods or prophets
could have meant for this
to be?

Nuclear

Sandra Cookson

Say "clear." Now say "new"
(as in nuked).
Now say "nuclear."

It seems ironic—
those who need
to say "nuclear" in public

can't pronounce the word.

Such a dangerous
word to stumble on:
whether
weapons, waste, or even energy
follow

Like a clumsy younger brother
leading his older down a dark street
marked "one way"

Bombs & Bread: A True Story

(from The U.S. in Afghanistan, 2001)

Sandra Cookson

Be careful, warn the leaflets
(an afterthought, no irony) fluttering

down with the bombs and the bread.
Be careful not to pick up

the yellow packet of unexploded bomblets,
mistaking it for the other yellow packet

that is food. Be careful!

to distinguish the stiff yellow rectangle of the bomb
should it land unexploded (some do)

from the softer yellow package that is food.
Don't try to pick up the bomb as if it were the
bread.

(P.S. Today they announced the good package will
now be *blue*)

proving again, as if we didn't know, that bombs &
bread does not compute.

From A Conscientious View

Orman Day

Guys born on my birth date, Feb. 12, 1946: Jack Beard, James Boyd, Harry Branham and 14 others.

Guys who shared my birthplace of Glendale, California: Allan Altieri, Richard Billingsley, Stephen Burlingame and 16 others.

From West Covina, where I received my draft notice: Harold Christensen, Charles Cook, Bert Guenther and nine others.

Sharing my first name: Orman Crossley, Orman Phillips and Orman Stone.

Sharing my last name: Arthur Day, Billy Day, Calvin Day and 19 other Days.

All of these guys have their names on the Wall, and sometimes I wonder if one of them is taking my place because I wouldn't go to the Vietnam War.

And, what of my two Glendale High classmates, Gary Nelson, a Marine killed in 1966, and Dick Klug, who was born not three weeks before me, was drafted into the Army and died of multiple fragmentation wounds in the summer of 1967?

I've done the calculus another way, too, and I've been comforted that the Wall doesn't include the name of the 42 draftees who reported with me to the Army reception center on March 15, 1970. Still, as world events make us recall that war, I contemplate the results of a moral decision I made when I was 22, and ask myself: Should my face be on a demon-haunted alcoholic sleeping beneath an underpass or on a paraplegic warehoused in the V.A.? Was it enough to refuse induction or should I have blocked troop trains with my body and set fire to selective service files? And what should I be doing now that our country is hoisting its flag again, muffling even the slightest dissent with cries of treason, and killing villagers in inhospitable terrains where good and evil are not easily identified?

Patriotism was defined simply during my boyhood in

conservative Glendale, the Southern California city where Marion Morrison starred on the local high school football team before he was renamed John Wayne and mowed down "Japs" and Nazis at Iwo Jima, Normandy Beach, and Bataan. If the nation called, guys did their duty…just as some of my friends' older brothers were doing theirs in the Korean conflict.

In our games of war—fought from fort to fort and backyard palm tree to backyard fig tree with toy guns and Army surplus gear—no boy ever waved two split fingers overhead and suggested that we give peace a chance.

I grew up revering the flag and the tenets of my church. When I was in third grade, I walked to First Methodist an hour before Sunday school and talked to the stained-glass image of the Boy Jesus shepherding his lambs. Sometimes I talked to my bust of Abraham Lincoln, too. I shared his Feb. 12 birthday, a holiday then, which meant that I was spared the birthday spankings—one swat for each year and a pinch to grow an inch—that other boys had to endure, pinned to the asphalt of the school playground.

Someone taught me not to lift my fists to fight in anger. Maybe it was my mom who could wound with a disappointed twist of her eyebrows if—roughhousing with a neighbor boy—our panting laughter shifted into angry grunts. Or maybe it was my dad, a gentle man who never raised a fuss outside the household. Or maybe it was Jesus, telling us to turn the other cheek. I battled my three sisters, of course, over TV shows and occupancy of the lone bathroom, but I never hit them with a closed fist.

Like virtually all of the children in Glendale, a "lily-white" city that kept blacks from residing within its boundaries through real estate covenants, I was raised to be a Republican who proudly promoted the election of Dwight Eisenhower and his running mate, Richard Nixon, by wearing an "I Like Ike" button on my t-shirt. By my senior year of high school, shaped by Carl Sandburg's voluminous biography of Lincoln and the preachings of the Methodist Youth Fellowship, I was an idealist and crusading newspaper editor who thought that America should live up to its responsibilities as the greatest country in the world. If our founding documents declared that all people are created equal, then we should treat them equally. Although my parents held racist ideas, they didn't keep me from performing an act that carried some risk: hosting two black teenage boys who were attending a youth conference at our church.

As editor of the Cal State Los Angeles paper in the spring and fall semesters of 1966, an era of growing student unrest, I saw that divergent and often controversial opinions about the Vietnam War were expressed in our pages. Still, I trusted President Johnson and his advisers when they told us that our country had a responsibility to save Indochina from becoming a domino toppled by the Communists. In an editorial for the campus paper, I wrote:

A friend of mine is dying. His death is a slow death. His is a bloody death. He has many foes: their swords have drawn many lashes. His enemy stalks him in the jungles of Africa, in the rice paddies of Vietnam, in the fields of South America and yet, also in the cities of America.

After calling for an offensive against the country's totalitarian foes and the internal weakness begotten by intolerance and immorality, I concluded:

Will my friend live or will he succumb as a "noble experiment?" You the individual are the answer to this question. You are his only guardian. Will you let him live? Or will you sentence him to Soviet gallows? You have the weapons. You must stand up and fight his battle.

A friend of mine is dying: his name—democracy.

While covering a weekend mountain retreat sponsored by the SDS (the Students for a Democratic Society), a New Left organization, I learned the techniques of non-violent civil disobedience: how to go limp if cops start to drag you to the squad car, how to protect your head and kidneys if bigots are kicking you when you're lying on the ground, how to use cigarettes to buy favors in jail…

When we viewed a grainy film that showed American bombing attacks on North Vietnam, some radicals cheered when a fiery U.S. fighter plane spiraled toward the earth. How, I wondered, could any American—no matter what their stance on the Vietnam War—take pleasure in the death of another American.

I left the mountain feeling no kinship with the other participants. Despite their platitudes about universal brotherhood, the SDSers seemed arrogant and self-centered. Maybe if I had worn sandals instead of tennis shoes.

As guys at school started to "feel the draft," my campus became the scene of teach-ins (hours-long discussions of the conflict) and silent vigils meant to pay homage to the dead. Rich Van Houten, my folk-singing partner, received his draft notice because he wasn't making "normal progress" toward completing his degree in four years at Cal State. He decided to enlist (adding another year to his stint) because he wanted to become a medic in a surgical unit instead of a grunt walking point on a forest trail threatened by snipers in the trees and Bouncing Bettys beneath the earth. I, myself, took 17 units.

I wrote an article about a faculty member who resigned her job because she was denied the opportunity to give her students credit or no credit marks at semester's end. "The teacher is placed in a morally intolerable position," she said, "if he or she realizes that the grade given to a student may influence not just whether the student will remain in school, not just whether the student will get a particular job, but also whether the student will be required to risk his life as a member of the armed forces."

Representing the paper, I joined a group of students who rode buses to San Francisco for a huge anti-war march. "It was a paisley stream of a march," I wrote. "Many hippies wore colorful outfits and flowers were held in soft hands and tucked behind ears of both sexes…An attractive wisp of a girl in tight, black pants and sweater had a sign—sewn onto the back of her upper garment—that read, 'Get out of Vietnam and into something cute.' The crowd carried thousands of signs that were all summed up by that of a big bear of a man: 'Get the hell out!'"

As an open-minded observer, I marched along with the 60,000 protesters, who were greeted with both peace signs and flipped fingers. In response to a group of hecklers, the monitor said, "Just ignore them. Everybody has a right to be sick."

I slept that night in a crowded basement, thanks to the hospitality of the Diggers, the "Salvation Army of the hippie set."

The door to the bathroom was a hunk of cardboard and the toilet was only to be flushed by every tenth person. As I wrote in my column, I was the ninth.

Still, although I was developing qualms about the war, I was ready to heed the call if I were drafted. At graduation in June 1967, I was accepted into VISTA, a national volunteer organization, which—though my motive was to use my education to help impoverished America—entitled me to a draft deferment for a year…enough time for peace to take shape. But, mononucleosis kept me from reporting to VISTA, which was going to send me to Oregon for training and then to Hawaii for my assignment. At the time, VISTA officials—I was told—thought that mononucleosis was a psychological disorder and I wasn't re-assigned. I found work as a cabin leader for the Los Angeles County outdoor school and at one point, anxious to get on with my life, wrote my selective service board to volunteer for the draft so I could do "my duty." The board replied that I'd have to fill out the paperwork in person at its Pasadena office, which was nowhere near the camp where I stayed weekdays.

Within months, I began to doubt the war. When news accounts chronicled the siege at Khe Sahn and the Tet offensive, America's military might no longer appeared invincible. And, more importantly, returned vets described to me the black markets selling stolen army supplies, the Saigon Cowboys (young Vietnamese men who avoided serving the very country that Americans were dying to protect), and the unreliability of the Vietnamese troops. The war, they said, was a big f——— joke and it was unwinnable, no matter what b.s. our government crammed down our throats.

Guys back from the war would invite my sisters and me to watch their slide shows and inevitably they'd show us a picture of themselves dangling the decapitated head of a suspected Viet Cong. At least no one showed us a severed ear that he had collected as a war trophy. None of the vets talked about defending democracy, but they had a lot to say about what a bargirl would do for a few bucks.

During the summer of 1968, a period in which police and National Guardsmen battled anti-war demonstrators at the Democratic National Convention in Chicago, I helped direct a YMCA summer camp on tranquil Catalina Island. I delivered campfire talks, collected funny tidbits for my "Corny Ormie" news reports, snorkeled and counseled campers about their faith. Every day I took time away from my duties to sit on the mountainside, praying for guidance and strength, and meditating by the lapping waves of the sea. That's when I felt that God was telling me not to kill for an unjust cause. I recognized that if ever I faced divine judgment, I couldn't shift the blame to my draft board because I shot a Vietnamese kid whose apple looked like a grenade or if I set fire to a hut with a Zippo and inadvertently burned to death a mama-san. Elsewhere, many fundamental Christians were hearing a different message: "Kill a commie for Christ." But that wasn't the Christ that I had come to know.

On that Catalina mountainside, I tried to sort through my choices. I wasn't willing to go to Canada or imitate other guys who were swallowing aluminum to mess up their X-rays or getting braces or losing lots of weight. And I wasn't going to say I was "queer" when I wasn't or go to the induction center and scream, "Gimme a gun! I wanna kill me some commies!" or enter the Army and wet the bunk night after night. I would stand up for my beliefs and accept the consequences, just like Abraham Lincoln, who nearly ended his political career by opposing the Mexican War as a congressman.

I decided that in this particular war I couldn't serve in the military in any role, even as a medic. Because I would defend my country and family if they were attacked, though, I didn't fit the legal definition of a conscientious objector (C.O.). I would make it clear to my draft board then that I wanted to perform alternative service (at a state mental hospital, for instance) as a C.O. based on my selective objection to the Vietnam War. In the end, I wanted my case to find its way to the Supreme Court, which I hoped would rule that men like me were being denied the free exercise of religion.

When I returned home from Y camp, I tried without success to gain a C.O. from my draft board through letters, forms, and a personal appearance. All of this I kept from my mom and dad because I wanted to spare them grief and worry as long as I could.

In February of 1969, with Richard Nixon now in the White House, I decided to satisfy my wanderlust and collect material for a novel by hopping freight trains out of Los Angeles. For a month, I endured some lonely, hungry, dangerous times and some exhilarating moments, too. In L.A.'s skid row, I flopped in rescue missions, picked carrots as a day laborer, and befriended ex-cons and petty hustlers by offering them a slug of Thunderbird. I developed a poker face and a kick-ass attitude, and nobody treated me like I was a tourist. Riding in boxcars, I walked in circles and stuffed newspapers into my clothes to keep warm. I got down to 15 cents in Utah and refused to hit anyone up for even a nickel. I slept on the floor of a New Orleans bus terminal with my shoes tied to my hands to thwart thieves. I only fought tears once, in Texas, on a bitterly cold night, when I had no place to stay and truckers wouldn't give me a lift. By the time I had thumbed back to West Covina, I was no longer afraid to go to prison.

To further prepare myself for incarceration, I read all the books I could on the subject, giving special attention to self-defense. Maybe I wouldn't defend the South Vietnamese government, but I had no qualms about shanking a con with a sharpened toothbrush to defend my backside in the shower.

I kept reading the same piece of advice: Do your own time. Don't get so involved with other inmates that you carry their burden or get in trouble because of their actions. You enter prison alone and you leave it alone…just like life. I decided I was going to start doing my own time immediately: I would speak to small groups and individual young men about my draft stand, but I wasn't going to be part of any anti-war organization. I didn't want someone claiming he was speaking for me and then cheer the downing of one of our pilots or call some hapless draftee a baby killer.

In an odd way, I was looking forward to prison, the way some guys looked forward to battle testing themselves. Inspired by Dostoevsky and Jean Genet, I expected to write about my experiences. I would probably be sent to Safford in Arizona with white-collar criminals, a relatively easy place to do my time. It wasn't going to be Devil's Island or Alcatraz, but I'd find a novel there somehow.

My appeals for C.O. status rose through the selective service bureaucracy and eventually reached the president himself. For months and months then, I would receive a rejection slip from a book publisher one day and from the government, the next.

Toward the end of 1969, my friend Rich came back from the war and grew a beard. His wife had left him and he was angry about the senseless deaths and mutilations that he had witnessed working in a surgical unit. And I wanted some freedom first if I was going to prison. So, we decided to hitchhike across the country, leaving with a penny each and folk-singing for our food and sleeping where we could for free. Rich restrung his guitar and to produce a tambourine, I painstakingly hammered a hundred bottle caps into a carved piece of wood.

Shortly before we left, the government conducted the era's first draft lottery. I sat before the family TV set on Dec. 1, 1969, knowing I would luck out if my number fell in the mid-200s or beyond. I watched the numbers and dates scroll up the screen. Sixty-eight…Feb. 12. I grunted a cuss word and snapped off the set. About 850,000 other guys cursed or celebrated that day. Bill Clinton was one of the lucky ones: his Aug. 19 birthday was No. 311.

A few weeks later, I quit my job as a child care teacher and started thumbing across America with Rich. I hoped that Nixon's "secret plan to end the war" would bear fruit before my draft notice fell into the family mail slot in West Covina. We zigzagged across the country, staying at a hippie commune in Taos, New Mexico, and trading songs with mountain folk in an Appalachian grocery store. Americans, I discovered anew, are generous people.

When Rich and I reached New Orleans, I sensed that the city's mood had shifted from the previous February when I had hopped freights to my first Mardi Gras. This year hippie types descended on Mardi Gras and the cops were out to bust them. A crowd gathered around Rich and me one evening when we started singing on a Canal Street corner. People were swaying and clapping and some guys started rocking a streetlight back and forth to our music. The cops came and told us to break it up. We did. Then one of the cops asked to see my homemade tambourine. I gave it to him and he said he was keeping it as a dangerous weapon. Some members of the crowd jeered the cops and we walked away. Halfway across Canal Street, Rich turned around and called the cops an obscene name. Moments later Rich and I felt hands tugging at our collars. When we were in a squad car, the cops turned on their siren because after they got us booked, they were off for the night.

At the New Orleans jail, we didn't have anything close to bail, so we were put in a holding tank, which was crowded with vomiting, crazed, angry guys. The place stank: the single toilet was stuffed up with the underpants of a guy who had lost control of his bowels when the cops beat him. With Rich trying to keep the din out of my ears with his hands, I phoned the chapter president of the national journalism society, of which I was a member, and pleaded with him to use his connections to get us free. He promised to do what he could.

After a few hours, Rich and I were separated because of a bureaucratic screw-up, and I ended up going to a cell in which more than a dozen guys were curled up in tormented sleep. I took the lone empty bunk, which was metal and didn't come with a blanket. I decided not to use the seat-less toilet because a guy was using the roll of toilet paper as a pillow and I didn't want to pull it out from under his head, given that I didn't know what charges he was facing.

I was lying there not looking forward to dealing with a bunch of potentially pissed-off cellmates when a jailer stood outside the bars and called my name. I was being released on my own recognizance, although I still had to go to trial two days later for reviling a police officer. At my trial, the officer lied and the judge couldn't ignore his contradictions and dismissed the charges. At his trial, Rich got off free because the officer didn't show up to testify. After my night in jail, though, I had no more romantic illusions about going to prison. I dreaded the claustrophobia…but not enough to cave in.

A few weeks later, a couple months into our trip, I phoned home from Virginia. My sister Laurel told me my draft notice had arrived and she had told our parents that I was going to refuse induction. Dad had wept—the first time she'd ever seen him cry—and said he hadn't raised me to be a traitor. Rich and I were thinking about continuing on to Europe, an act that would've meant certain imprisonment when I came back, but my family wanted me to come home and so I did.

At the induction center in L.A., I first had to pass the physical. I had a bashful kidney and couldn't relax to give a urine specimen, so I asked the guy next to me if he had diabetes and when he said no, I asked him for some of his sample. Finally, all of us were led into a large room to take our oaths. I refused to step forward when I was asked to take my place in the U.S. Army. For spiritual support, I gripped a pocket-sized Gideon Bible—a gift given all of us by a Red Cross worker—open at Matthew to "Blessed are the peacemakers..." The other guys were led away to buses for the ride to basic training and I went home and resumed my part-time job working with disabled children at a recreation program.

I had no idea how the FBI was going to arrest me. Would they lead me away from the family home in fetters? Would they pull me out of the swimming pool when I was teaching a kid with muscular dystrophy how to swim? Two months after my refusal, an FBI agent phoned me when I was visiting one of my sisters. He said I could go to FBI headquarters on my own or I could be picked up. I drove myself to Los Angeles and posed for mug shots with a placard full of numbers hanging around my neck. As hard as I tried, I couldn't put a yearbook smile on my lips. The FBI sent me home and told me I'd be hearing from the federal judicial system, whose dockets were becoming clogged by the growing numbers of resisters such as myself.

That October, when I went on trial in the Los Angeles courthouse, my sisters—expecting Perry Mason for the defense—were aghast when they saw that my attorney wore a ponytail. Before the federal district court judge, I explained my views and then because I didn't deny committing the crime, the U.S. attorney chose to let the facts speak for themselves. This was not going to be "Inherit the Wind." During the trial, I learned through his comments that the judge was a fellow Glendale High graduate and Methodist, and had helped build the YMCA camp where I had been a director. While he found me guilty of refusing induction into the armed forces, he sentenced me only to a year of unsupervised probation.

The price of my stand was relatively mild: probation, attorney fees that could've bought me a couple of used VW Beetles, a seven-year postponement of my journalism career and lifelong sorrow over my dad's humiliation and grief. My punishment, I understand, pales compared to the price paid by resisters who were imprisoned and reluctant draftees who returned from the front zippered into body bags.

Still, I was a felon and because of a decision by my attorneys not to appeal, I wasn't going to change the law for others. I was free, but I wasn't...even after I was pardoned by President Ford as part of an amnesty program for resisters, evaders and deserters...a program probably meant to appease liberals who criticized him for pardoning Nixon for his Watergate crimes.

A few years ago, a guest column in *Newsweek* was written by a man whose brother—an Air Force captain—killed himself after returning home from North Vietnam, where he spent seven brutal years as a POW. The author blamed those of us who protested the war for his brother's descent into despair. Seeking a scapegoat for his brother's suicide, he demonized all war opponents by burdening us with the actions of those few, highly publicized extremists who waved Viet Cong banners, spat on returning veterans and branded them as "murderers." That's like characterizing all veterans as dope-crazed psychos.

The author wrote that his "brother had no say in the politics that sent him to war." That's not entirely true. No one forced him to join the Air Force and become a captain. No one forced him to fly a plane over enemy villages. Of course, the pilot didn't want to bomb churches and hospitals or hate the North Vietnamese or become a killer. He only wanted to be an astronaut. But he didn't resist commands to bomb and kill. He did his own time and he suffered the consequences.

I don't want to be cruel, but I'm getting angry at the repeated efforts of certain conservatives to rewrite the history of that accursed conflict, trying to turn Saigon Cowboys and black marketers into freedom fighters. If they want to make me feel guilty about the names on the Wall, they've failed. When I walk past those names, I only feel rage. Anti-war protesters and journalists didn't keep America from conquering an army of peasants determined to end decades of foreign domination and create a fairer form of government. When younger guys talk to me about the war, none of them are even aware of fraggings...how U.S. soldiers killed and wounded hundreds of their own unpopular officers with explosive devices and rifle shots to the back. They think we could've won if only our planes had dropped more bombs, 8 million tons not being sufficient.

Now all of us can only grieve for the souls lost and bodies disfigured by that war—both American and Vietnamese—and by the war that is being waged in Iraq. Peace is eluding us again and young guys...and even young women...may be forced to make choices that could put them in prison or etch their names into a wall. They'll have to do their own time...just like the guys in my generation.

Report From the Front

Juditha Dowd

Someone has crushed the stars again
and all that now inflames the sky
is the brutal anger of Mars.

I've ridden his back reluctantly
and I want him dimmed tonight
as I lie on my belly, beetle-shaped

trapping sleep like a dirty prize.
What beneficent god would have set us here
to fall upon each other

like dogs abandoned on an island,
every living thing as prey?
The stars—

let someone restore them,
the One who would protect them,
who doesn't know us.

I refuse to call His name.
Out here, the sky kicked open,
we lie beneath the floorless room of night.

War Toys

Alexander Levering Kern

Escaping news of war
for once, I seek the peace
that only a forest knows

yet even here a sandy bar
divides the reservoir
and through the trees

I hear the steady
thunk thunk thunk
of ancient stone on brittle wood

as children laugh with glee
and fashion from fallen trees
their weapons of war.

Granite boulders lie quietly,
scarred by fire, strewn by ice
as the sun bleeds slow and scarlet
across the western sky.

Wing Man of the Gulf

-for Petty Officer Third Class Stephen K. Rand

James Gage

I can only begin to imagine
what you first understood
on those blast iron floors of the ship
with surveillance photos
splayed out like ordnance,
like the flat death
they would later
become. Did your mind

flash for an instant to some distant memory,
some nursery rhyme moment
forgotten from youth?
Did your twenty-two years
begin to feel like a sieve,
like some filter for existence
with no clear beginning and without any end?

In the recruitment office
you hadn't heard the word *death*
but of course there were signs,
and the synonyms replayed in your mind
what you hoped you could be:
heroic and brave, invincible, best.
War was just an abstraction;
a stop-cycle thought that happened
to somebody else, but then
there you were:

green and clean-shaven:
coordinate-seeker, eye-
dropper of bombs.

In your nursery-room dreams
did the sheep have brave faces
as they met their demise, and did they have names?
Did they bleat out real words as they
moved between worlds in that deja-vu instant
before the sky was blot out?
What was then left

to replace the small word
that has no earthly meaning,
and what could be done with the nothing that
     remained?
What could be gleaned from history's lesson
unlearned, and what shape would it take—
this divisive and spiteful,

utter blindness of
faith?

Happy Hour

Jerry Judge

Iraq battle scenes
no longer captivate
this crowd as a brunette

in a tailored blue suit
orders barkeep to switch channels
or turn off the carnage before

it ruins the chicken dinner
she'll soon be picking up
on her way home to the condo.

The bartender hops to the TV
on his one good leg.
He turns the sound up.

Coming Home

Kelly Cunnane

One of my island friends holds a party for the 21-year old on a short leave after nine months in Iraq. I shudder, thinking of how the town held the Fourth of July fireworks to coincide with his arrival home, how much they sound like bombs, look and smell like a war I've never seen.

At the party, people are playing basketball in the driveway, milling about on the lawn. Out back, the garage door is open, pool table in use, coolers of beer, a table sagging with chips and dip.

I'm personally not wild about the boy returning from Iraq, simply because my daughter from age 15 to 16 snuck around with him; he's old enough to drink and does, and drives a brilliant yellow truck too fast, swears, and basically was too old, too callous, and – I could not point that out clearly enough – she was smitten.

So, I was the only person who was relieved when he was shipped out, no longer available, no longer within my daughter's one - way hormonal vision. Email seemed less troublesome.

Yet, I also felt acutely for the boy. He had signed up at age 17, the financial support for further education, the lure. Further education here on the island is still a relatively new phenomenon; that he, the son of a lobsterman, was actually attending school was new and good for the island, and for the young man too. That he was pulled out with less than a year to go seemed counterproductive to me. Made me wince.

"He signed up for the Army," people pointed out, "Took the paycheck sure enough… so what's the big shock?" And yet, it was. That someone I knew was leaving everything he knew to go to war gave me pause. Even if he were too old for my daughter.

The returning soldier strikes me as more angular, a part of him perpetually taut, something harshly attentive emerging from beneath his skin, almost as if still attuned to war. The part of him that grips a rifle continues without it, unable to hear the "at ease" command, his body trained, knowing too much we do not.

"By Jesus," the soldier says, genuinely impressed that the mother who didn't want him hanging around with her daughter is coming across the lawn to welcome him home. We hug. His arms, his torso feel hard.

"Would you like the No-Bakes in your truck or to share?" I ask, balancing the cookie sheet of chocolate cookies on my fingertips.

"In the truck," he says promptly, as if people will take them as we speak. His eyes are round, fingers already reaching. "Said you'd send 'em, never did," he says.

"I was going to send them," I say, "but here you are!" He thanks me, and I put them in his yellow truck and see why my daughter might have been smitten simply by the interior of his gleaming pick-up.

"The truck just might be worth the job in the Army," I say, everyone knowing his pay went to the truck.

The boy looks far away and blank. His wise-guy affability struggles to come home, tries to find its way back, make sense of the layer of war that has cut it in half, made being a wise-guy suddenly a useless tool that once worked so well in governing himself around the island where he grew up, the rough mainland where he cruises, drinks, finds girls.

Kids are leaping on a new yard trampoline. Men are drinking rum. Dusk comes in sweeps of salty fog, the bay beyond. A heap of wooden palettes is beginning to roar in the backyard by the shore. Sparks heave up into the sky and darkness reigns, the kids on the trampoline white shirts bouncing up then down.

"Never thought I'd be keeping you in my prayers," I tell him. He nods. Tells us standing in the yard that his first month in Iraq he received 87 letters. Says they kept him going.

The woman who's having the party apologizes for not writing.

"I wrote to tell him to come home safely but not to date my daughter," I say, and they laugh. "So," I say searching his face, "Anything good at all about Iraq? Any children?" He's from the island, a place where people like children. A lot.

"Yeah," he drawls, and I almost have time to say, Good, and tell him how I always thought he had a way with children when he adds, "They were shooting at me." His I-don't-give-a-crap laugh doesn't find sound, his face like plastic surgery.

"I'm sorry," I say. And shrink at how incredibly naïve I am compared to this boy.

"They hate us," he says.

"You must hate them now."

"I do."

Later, when people have moved out back and are well into their beer and rum, their personalities altered, and the dark is so dark that it's hard to identify the children jumping on the trampoline, can't tell who is who, and the pool game is going, and it's come clear that the girl sitting alone, not speaking, gliding from bathroom to a hunched spot on the lawn, is a new girlfriend from away that the soldier has brought along, and the fire is roaring and the mosquitoes biting fiercely, it's then that I see, out from the corner of my eye, the boy turn around, his head bowed as he stands back-to at the fringe of the party. I look away, thinking he's urinating. When I look again, he's still back-to, his head bowed as if a tremendous weariness beyond weariness has settled there. He is not a weeping kind of person. And yet, I know he is weeping.

His father appears, and he takes the boy into a large embrace that is at once subtle and mighty. The embrace both protects his son's privacy, no one seems to notice, and does something I have never in my life witnessed between men; it comforts the boy. The father's face burned from lobster fishing is wet, his arm strong around the boy.

An uncle, a friend, and then another friend appear. No women, no one even looking, and the boy is in a couch of men on the fringe of a drunken party, the white shirts of the children going up in the dark, the new girlfriend hugging her knees, my daughter down by the enormous fire trying to make sense of the boy's indifference, his bowed and embarrassed back as he stands for a long, long time and the men are there, holding him, his back to us, his head bowed, in the circle of men.

Pacifist Salutes the Passing Veteran

Alice Bolstridge

1. First Love

    1949, in the school hall you hug me;
    eleven years old, I carve a heart
    on my desk with our initials. Teased,
    I scratch it out before I turn twelve.
    1955, we approach and retreat again.
    You begin your army life. We marry others.
    Briefly, rarely, we greet each other in passing
    through the years. 1998, we declare love,
    but you have other commitments,
    and our declaration, as speech does, floats
    in the air across the distance between us,
    another aborted story.   September 2003,
    you come home to say goodbye, cancer,
    three to six months, four already gone.

2. Terminal Effects

    This time, after you leave, we talk every day
    on the phone through the fall. Reviewing
    our history, we tell of failed marriages,
    children, grandchildren, great grandchildren,
    long solitude, attempts to find love
    so brief and long ago we can't remember
    the names of some.   In late October,
    you tell me about standing outside barefoot
    in the frosty morning, feeding wild turkey,
    squirrels, chickadees, and feeling in your toes
    the first tingling, side effects of this last
    drug trial to treat the terminal effects
    of Agent Orange and other war wounds
    and stresses of your army life.

3. War History

My memory of childhood reality
is scanty, but this dream from the early 40s
is crystal clear: little yellow men with slanted eyes,
like those from comics, come at me with bayonets
pointing, growing bigger and bigger. Closer
and closer they come while I try to work
my jaw to scream, my legs to run, but I
am numb, can't even wake up when I try.
After, the dream comes without sleeping,
through Korea, Viet Nam, the Gulf,
Kosovo, and here it comes again. War
was everyday stuff in your long work life.
For me, it is the stuff of nightmares,
ideals, stories and poems—all in my head.

4. Weather Forecast

You say, *The wind is coming your way*.
All the tamaracks have turned orange here,
and moose are on the move. At dawn and dusk,
they herd in the alfalfa field to feed.
I counted 12 one morning. Neighbors
say they saw as many as 18. Their coats shine;
the bulls' muscles bulge for the battles of rutting.
The winds wake me at 2:30 in the morning
I listen a while, then go out to look.
Black clouds rush across the still night blue.
Venus is huge. I imagine waves of our love
riding out on the wind to meet each other. I dream
of us swimming—creatures without history,
we glide over and around each other.

5.   School Work

It's nearing the end of fall term;
literature students are finishing projects
and anxious about conclusions.
Back in September, I asked the many
who were having trouble with war stories,
Why did you choose the topic?
Some wanted to see what happens
to human character in extreme conflict.
Some wanted to review the history of war.
Some wanted to explore ideals—
courage, honor, love of freedom,
democracy, country. One, destined
already for the Navy, didn't know why.
No one mentioned fear of the Iraq war.

6.   Natural History

Those beautiful young bodies—I want
to snatch them all up, carry them away
to a safe place where they can research
nature's stories, watch closely the pair
of bald eagles I saw last week flying circles
of approach and retreat around each other.

But there are no safe places,
and salvation is not in my job description.
Instead, I prod them to think more deeply
about the weight of *The Things*
They Carry, to analyze more closely
the *Quiet on the Western Front.* Some
think now that conclusions are impossible
and wish they had chosen another topic.

7.   Special Topics

I post a course description for Special Topics
in May: <u>War, Peace, and Patriotism</u>. Next day,
I get 2 e-mails from a colleague, retired vet.
One, addressed to all teaching staff, asks,
What professional ethics should guide talk
with students about the Iraq war? The other
is addressed to me: A. Your May Term
sounds interesting. Tell me more: the approach
the principles, the resources. It may be similar
to my Ethics course. Perhaps we can "deconflict." T.

T., Students choose the content.   I use the Socratic
method and play devil's advocate on all sides.
I express my opinions, uncertainties,
and efforts to understand the ethics. Sincerely, A.

8.   Deconflicting ?

A. I'm afraid I left the wrong impression.
I also add my two cents, but it seems best
to avoid "asserted conclusions." It's unethical
to push an agenda. The value to our students
is not our conclusions but process
and rationale. Does that make sense?   T.

T. Sure. All my moral certainties get fractured
by reality, so it's hard to "assert conclusions."
Still, I push agendas—for honesty, respect, work,
love. And peace. I'm not troubled by overt agendas.
It's the covert ones that leave me worrying.
Do we agree? What do you think? Respectfully, A.

His classroom is just two doors down the hall.
We greet in passing, but we don't talk about this.

9.   Love Letter 1

November *National Geographic*
has a feature about studies of the skin.
Cultures that express love with lots of touch
have lower levels of aggression.
Not able to touch you, my heart melts
when I think of you, it's turning to syrup.
3 months is not enough time to say
goodbye. I want years and years. I want
to walk with you in the woods, sunlight
filtering through the leaves, leaving you
dappled with shadows. I want
to eat watermelon with you and lick
the juice from your chin. I want to watch
romantic comedies and laugh so hard I cry.

10.   Love Letter 2

I want to hear all your stories you
haven't been able to tell me yet.
I want to talk and talk and talk until
we are all talked out. Then I want to lie
by your side with my ear on your chest
and listen to your heartbeat and breath.
I want to sleep with you, skin to skin,
until the sun comes up.

                    Sometimes,
just when I think I can't stand this distance,
your love blows over me like a breeze
from the South over April slush.
I woke up this morning with it
warming my bed, a happy place.

11. Celebrating the King of Peace

During Christmas break, I drive south to visit
you for six days. In spaces between pain,
we walk and cook and eat and talk of work
and love and war. You have lived so long
in my lost and forgotten self, I am
greedy to know all I'll never know of you.

I ask, What did you like about soldiering?
I was good at it. Every mission was dangerous,
    and every minute I was facing death
I felt more alive than any other time.
But I advised my son not to do it,
and I don't like this war my grandson will fight.

We go to bed early to savor
the long touch of our sleeping.

12. Happy Ending

All it takes for a happy ending
is to stop the story in a happy place,
and I have work waiting back home,
so we say Goodbye again, agreeing
to make it short. But it follows me
all the way up I 81 along
the Smoky Mountains, through fog
and misty rain, through a storm
that strands me for an extra day,
through a fairyland of snow
glittering in bright sun from trees
and rolling farmland. I try hard to weave
the beauty of it all into this story,
to make of it some consolation.

13. Super Earth

> In calls, our Goodbye lingers into February.
> Finally you say, *I'm going to ground*.
> Super Earth is the hardest Go to Ground
> for terriers bred to work quarry in dens
> or tunnels underground. Spring, 1999,
> about the Kosovo war, a headline reads
> "NATO need not go to ground yet."
> Another story, Winter 2002: "Jewels of antiquity
> go to ground." Trying to save history from bombs,
> they bury ancient artifacts in secret places.
> After the capture of Khalid Sheikh Mohammad,
> reporters talk of terrorists going to ground.
> In flashback tunnels, Vietnam Vets still go to
>   ground.
> *It's time*, you repeat, *for me to go to ground*.

14. March

> Another blizzard with white-out winds
> and drifting so strong police order drivers
> off the road. I dream I look for you
> through the blinding snow in Area 51,
> that top secret military base
> which inspires so many stories
> of UFOs and extra-terrestrials.
> I go so far to ground I get lost,
> and still I can't find you. Once again,
> our human family fails the love command,
> and winds of war come with storms
> of ancient rituals—pathos and drama,
> power passions, and blood sacrifice
> going all the way to ground.

The Cinematic Genius of Alexander Korda

Julie Lechevsky

It is good to die in Baghdad at nineteen,
while thieves are looting the antiquities,
stuffing their pockets with cylinder seals,
as though they were tootsie rolls for a matinee.
It puts me in mind of *The Thief of Bagdad*
with Sabu playing the title role,
meeting the blind beggar in prison
(really Prince Almad) and saying:
"I am Abu the Thief. Son of Abu the Thief.
Grandson of Abu the Thief."
Who would not want his role in life
clearly established from youth?

Later, after their escape from prison,
and dalliance with a beautiful princess
(played by June Duprez),
they stand before an impenetrable cave
while magic carpets whirr above them and say the magic
    words:
**WEAPONS OF MASS DESTRUCTION-RELATED
    PROGRAM ACTIVITIES**
and, lo, the cave clanks open,
and they go in for the gold.

I wanted to die in the balcony of the *Lyric,*
not as an expert on old movies,
but at the height of ignorance and hope,
still dependent on genies.
This tour of the Tigris will have to do instead.
My mother will be pleased:
I could have been a milkman

driving through the summer,
lightly leaping from the cab with bottles,
or a security guard at Corning.
What kind of jobs are they?
Now Mother can think of me as a military man,
hero and virgin in khakis,
and all the things I might have been still possibilities.
Never a low paying job, never a real girl.
The marvelous cave opens.
I seize on anonymity as though it were a pearl.

Fruits of the Crimean War

Joanne Lowery

Because the major powers of Europe
rushed to protect Christians from Turkish infidels
the military first learned to use the telegraph
to expedite orders to kill

and the Minié rifle proved its bullet
could burrow so effectively from afar
that soldiers would no longer have to stand
close together blackened with smoke

and clever undersea mines blew up steamships
while engineers built trenches two generations
before the rats and mud of World War I
and invented telescopes to look up over the top

and thousands of schoolchildren
including one in Mrs. Gates' sixth grade class
in northern Ohio, 1956, memorized
Tennyson's galloping poem about courage

or disaster and from every war before
to every war after how the world
especially northern Ohio was a better place.

Old Folks Grow Silent (Villanelle)

Elaine Morgan

Old folks grow silent in a mindful way.
Wars turn into floral wreaths and names on stone.
Will young folks smile and nod one day?

Outer passions dim with time old folks say.
Another taste of war makes dry tongues groan.
Old folks grow silent in a mindful way.

Youth fights to keep its country's enemies at bay.
Spills precious blood on foreign shores away from home.
Will young folks smile and nod one day?

Once a year they bend their knees and heads to pray.
For strangers and for those whose names are known.
Old folks grow silent in a mindful way.

Age seeks and finds one final enemy to slay.
The war becomes a myth, the death a metered poem.
Will young folks smile and nod one day?

The inner battlefield a silent, bloodless fray.
The call to arms a thoughtful Buddhist koan.
Old folks grow silent in a mindful way.
Will young folks smile and nod one day?

Eyewitness

David Radavich

Softness has left
to take up residence

somewhere else.

That was another soul
than the one I was born with,

another world
than we know without
looking.

I wish
life were otherwise

I wish

I could report tuna casseroles
and tiaras, a babe

in a manger
taken in by strangers,

visits by wise people who traveled far
to locate their blessings,

seers who avoid going home to routines
they know only kill and maim

I wish

the front lines

rhymed into stanzas

that a superior poet
could freeze into beauty

that would equal
truth

leap into joy

give us back
comforting news

tomorrow and tomorrow

However War

Yvette A. Schnoeker-Shorb

We think we know this time
where we are going,
what we are going to get,
how we are going to get it
and why.

But war writes itself;
we find our roles,
deleting everything
except what we need
to fight.

Lake Carnegie, Late Afternoon

Nancy Scott

Orange sky
slips below the tree line.
College oarsmen, stroke by stroke,
slice ever-graying water.

On the road, arms awhirl,
a legless man, wheelchair-bound,
placard round his neck
— *I'm a homeless Vet.*

All race against the fading light,
resolute on course.
One outwitting midnight's chill,
others to the boathouse.

Herman Sharp *(1899-1918)*

Nancy Scott

My great uncle was killed at Argonne,
his body buried in foreign soil.
For its first hometown casualty,
Maywood created a park,
inscribed his name in bronze.
Other wars, more dying.
The ground was renamed Veterans Park.
No relative was there to protest
and children who swing on the swings
don't wonder.

Today the only proof I have of his life
is a faded photo postcard.
He's posing in front of a fake cannon,
the Capitol painted as background.
Crisp uniform, broad smile.
His buddy close at his side.
The message: *Dear Mom and Dad.*
See the new watch on my wrist.
How many hours, days until
innocence fell to artillery fire.

Internecine

J. D. Smith

Brother takes up arms against brother
And he who survives must face himself.

Still Life with Tank

J. D. Smith

There is a neutered tank
that won't bombard
or crush again.

The highest point for a hundred meters,
the tank has earned its rest,
which has just begun.

The barrel tells ten o'clock at all hours,
the turret lies open like a jagged can,
but rust has barely touched it.
The body could still be sold as scrap.

There is a neutered tank,
its turret open like a can,
its barrel trained on ten o'clock,
the highest point for a hundred meters.

There is no clock-tower or steeple.
There is a plaza filled with space.

There are good-enough foundations, with few
     cracks,
and cellars that could support new homes.

There is a neutered tank,
gun trained on ten o'clock..

There are good-enough foundations, lightly
     cracked,
and cellars that would support new homes.

There is a cemetery, obsolete or redundant,
overrun with weeds.

Among them, and around them,
mines rest like seeds that rise
to stalk and red flower
in a single footstep's season.

The War Cinquain

Morgan Grayce Willow

Twenty-
two syllables
can't contain the crack in
my soul. War, like ice in sidewalks,
breaks me.

II

MR. ROGERS IS DEAD, THE NEIGHBORHOOD IS SCARY

Mr. Rogers Is Dead

Pam McAllister

Mr. Rogers is dead and gone.
His sweet puppets are mute.
His sweater hangs forlorn on its hook.
It's a scary day in the neighborhood.

Now a daddy with tight lips and deaf ears
wants us to be his puppets.
Instead of a sweater,
he wears cowboy boots and a cowboy hat.
He's got "homeland security" guns for the boys
    and girls
and he's letting them ride the trains all they want.
He's hoping we'll tell on each other.
See anything suspicious? he asks, winking.
He's letting kids play in the sandbox far from home
and laughs when they knock down other kids'
    castles.

Mr. Rogers is dead and gone,
and it's a scary day in the neighborhood.

Twenty on 20

Lisa Bernardini

"An extremely small, microscopic number,"
said Ward. A. Campbell,
death penalty proponent,
of twenty exonerations from death row.
But consider,
sitting at a red light
through twenty cycles,
the drycleaner ruining
twenty shirts,
handing keys to a driver
with twenty DUIs,
catching the President
in twenty lies (bad example),
falling in love with a man
with twenty ex-wives,
being served a bowl of soup
with twenty flies,
reading any book by Faulkner,
or even just one sentence,
twenty times.

An Ohio Death

Columbus, July 1959

John E. Simonds

How slick the notion, speed the arc,
electricity would do the job.
Drink lots of water,
make yourself a good conductor,
they said the prison guards advised,
to make the current travel faster
all the way from head to knee.
Pudgy, bald in denims cut away at knee,
the prisoner, well accompanied, arrives.
Well, so long, captain. No hard feelings,
shaking the hand of the guard in charge.
The priest with his mantra,
The Lord is my Shepherd…
Praying at the last,
the Act of Contrition
came out with short breaths.
Oh, my God. I am heartily sorry…
filtered through black rubber mask.
We the witnesses stood to watch,
conducting ourselves as such,
guardians of the ceremonial light
conveyed from others gone before.
The death of Walter Byomin,
victim No. 311 of Ohio's chair.
Shooting a cop in Lorain
gave him little wiggle room,
yet the case survived for years,
building its own folklore within
the disinfectant walls and buzzer-

sounding waiting space of fright.
How slick the rounded faces neatly hung,
composite rows on chamber walls,
a portrait oval vacant for the latest guest.
A total photo record of their passing
water from the body, puddle on a rubber sheet
that lay beneath the chair.
A nod by the warden, Ralph Alvis,
a large and kindly football man,
an opponent of death but a penal pro
who'd nodded 50 times before
to people at the switches.
Two thousand volts made the subject lurch,
another 2000 and then ...
A doctor with stethoscope listens,
mopping upchuck from a purpling chest.
The body's rubber-veiled head
tilts to the side with thumbs
askew as claws against restraint.
Looking at his watch, the doctor notes the end.
Walter Byomin is dead— July 3, 1959.
A complete sentence – and more.
The lore of the chair laces
a web of wood and leather
and irony too rich to believe.
How slick the notion of inmate Justice,
who with carpentry skills built the chair,
served to his freedom, and later –
convicted of murder, died in its arms.
How slick the fable and the notion of deterrence.
William Sydney Porter did a stretch
and maybe got his marquee pen name
from the shingle (OHio pENitentiaRY).

True? Call it a theory,
as in the days and nights of Columbus,
alive with myths of discovery.
How slick the notion
in this central land of varnished pioneers,
a world of Columbian legend and O. Henry end-
    ings
with harsh half-truths
and arcing arcane possibilities,
so certain retribution works
with deadly force unfailing
and without mistake.

Excessive Punishment

Adrian S. Potter

Earl wasn't very bright; his IQ hovered near forty-five. Even getting dressed in the morning was a chore. If nobody prepared an outfit for him the night before, Earl would lumber downstairs mismatched, wearing both plaid and stripes. Shirts were sometimes buttoned inside out and boots were often associated with the wrong foot. Despite his fashion challenges, he always had fun. He loved to watch movies with other people, rocking side to side while trapped in a cinematic trance. Earl could easily memorize and recite dialogue from films, yet he struggled with the concept of tying his shoelaces.

Earl had also mastered using silverware at the dinner table, but his hands rarely wielded anything more menacing than a butter knife. That was what confused the investigators. One day, he was found stained in crimson, crying on a neighbor's stoop. Earl didn't understand that his father's heart had ceased beating, and he couldn't explain why he was grasping a bloody Ginsu blade.

For this he was given an injection. To help him take a long nap, like they told Earl right before he was strapped onto a gurney. I guess that's why laws exist, to rid our society of a thirty-year- old murderer whose final words were "*I wanna watch cartoons.*"

The Understanding

Adrian S. Potter

It seemed harmless at first. They were just another cluster of corporate clones, seven mid-life crisis victims enjoying happy hour. It looked like a light beer commercial. They were fully engaged in happy chitchat; you assumed it was about fatherhood or fantasy football.

You proceeded over to their table, but only because it was your job. You jotted down their order, some expensive microbrews with lemon wedges. The talking and snickering resumed once you left. You wondered what was so hilarious, but you ignored them.

The problem with being a good listener is that you often pay attention to things that you aren't intended to hear. While you were tending to a mess at a nearby table, one of the men clearly said, "Two niggers walk into a bar…"

They were making racial jokes. Your ethnicity was a punch line in their personal comedy special. You glared at the business-men, your body wrapped in a cocoon of shock. And they continued on laughing, laughing like their ancestors did when they whipped your ancestors, laughing like they would consider shackling your black ass if that pesky 13th Amendment hadn't been ratified.

One guy eventually sensed your anger and apologized with the transparent sincerity of a politician. The others quieted down while you shook his hand with all the professionalism you could muster. You bitterly retreated to the bar and poured their drinks, contemplating giving your manager two weeks notice.

While you wiggled each mug slightly so that your nigger saliva would mix perfectly with their premium beers, a childhood memory came to mind. Your dad had once said, "Never work where you have to take other people's bullshit with a smile."

At that moment you understood exactly what your father meant.

Last Luck

R. Yurman

*"Good fortune deriving from
the final bit of anything."*
Dialect of Leeds, 1862

(for Trisha)

You hand a plastic takeout container,
leftovers from your expensive dinner,
to the woman rocking
in her cocoon of blankets
on the corner outside Opera Plaza.
This assures you
a brilliant future –

as giving a child
the core of an apple
bestows fruitfulness
upon the giver.

What the receiver gets,
beyond a couple of mushy bites
and a handful of seeds,
is quite another matter.

*(Based on the entry for March 11, 2004 in "Forgotten English"
A Daily Calendar, Produced by Jeffrey Kacirk)*

Counter-Terror

R. Yurman

*"(with respect to aliens overseas) there is no
obligation under the Convention Against Torture …"*
— Alberto Gonzales, U.S. Attorney General
Designate, Senate Confirmation Hearings

"Nothing's learned by turning away"
— Ellen Bryant Voigt

The tip of an electric needle
Lovingly applied to the soft
Core of a woman or a man
Lips gums tongue anus genitals
Will produce the results desired

We study the most effective techniques
Teach them for use on foreign soil
Exported prisoners
Exotic hands on the dials

Watch the news over dinner
Squirming human piles photographed
By female guards who poke their nakedness
Then feign sex with dogs
A nightly peep show for all of us
No sharp edges no downward spiral

Terazin

On visiting a Nazi holding camp in Czech Republic

Elizabeth Weir

Above the iron gate, "Arbeit Macht Frei."
Like those before, we walk beneath the lie,
Ken, myself, Vashek, Vlosda and little Kuba.
We pass the bare washroom, built to impress
credulous inspectors from the Red Cross,
see sheds for forced labor; punishment cells.
We walk through blocks stacked with bunks—
fathers, mothers, children, all separated,
the children shipped away early to the East.
We step over weed-choked railroad tracks

to a crescent of uncut grasses. Kuba
drops his mother's hand and skips
ahead to a hillock of wild flowers.
We watch him gather ox-eye daisies
until his hands are full. "Dada," he calls,
holding up his bouquet. Vashek hesitates,
caught in the past, then he drops to one knee
and knots the stems with a stalk
of reed-canary grass and Kuba runs
to give his mother the present.

Pointe du Hoc, Normandy

Elizabeth Weir

I
The sea-wind chills me at the cliff's edge.

II
Omaha Beach lies west. Utah stretches east.
A farmer blades dark weals into damp earth.
White gulls glide in the plow's slow wake.
Beyond a bramble hedge, a cow, square
as a Panzer tank, chews her cud.

III
I think of our two American sons.

IV
On this cliff-top, young American soldiers
knocked out a six-gun German battery
embedded in steel and concrete.
An Atlantic storm pounded high seas
into the swollen Channel. Landing vessels
blew off course. Some sank. Young men
crabbed over sea-slammed rocks, scrambled
up the cliff's tall jut. Support fire hurtled above.
German grenades exploded around them.
Injured boys fell to the rocks below.
The survivors climbed on. They took
the promontory and held it, tearing metal
ahead, the sheer drop behind.

V
At my feet, two field poppies, petals
still crumpled from the bud's
tight pack, shiver in the salty up-draft,
fragile crimson tissue.

In My Image

Aida K. Press

I am the Lord, thy God
And only I have created
Woman and man in my image.
Whatsoever I doeth is holy and righteous.

If the man loveth the woman
And the woman loveth the man
That is good in my sight.

And if the woman loveth the woman
And the man loveth the man
Is that not also good?

If the man or the woman
Raise up children
And love them
And bring them up
In My ways
That is good.

And if they
Invite the hungry
To sup at their table
And to warm themselves
At their hearth

And if they give clothes
To the ragged
And comfort the lost
And the bereaved

And if they teach their children
To do righteous deeds
They do my work on earth.

The nay-sayers
You who appoint yourselves
Judge and jury
You are the accursed.
You who think

You are holier than the holy
Who sneer at the union
Of a man and a man

Or a woman and a woman
Know that I have created them
And if you cast them out
You cast out me

For I am woman and man
And as it is with me
So be it on earth
For all humankind.

City of Peace

Aida K. Press

Beloved, do you remember the last time we
went up to Jerusalem? It was only a few years ago
that we walked along the Promenade,
the City of David behind us
and across the valley
the golden Dome of the Rock
gleaming in the evening sun.
That morning we posed
for a photograph in the courtyard
of the El Aksa mosque, our arms around
each other's shoulder, when the Arab guard
rushed over to us. "No touching bodies,"
he said. "No touching bodies."

And do you remember the day we strolled
along the crooked streets of the Old City
where the church, the synagogue,
and the mosque huddle together
and the chants of the three faiths
rise equally up to heaven?

And the noisy streets crowded with tiny shops
where we fed each other fresh pomegranates
the juice staining our lips and fingers ruby red.
And the little jewelry shop where you
haggled over the price of the silver
and amber necklace before you
triumphantly presented it to me.

Beloved, let us cherish the memory
of those peaceful days
before little children were blown
up in the streets,
whole families assassinated
at a Passover seder,
shoppers bombed
as they bought food for the Sabbath,
men and women ousted
from their homes at gunpoint,
their houses demolished,
and let us have faith
that days of peace
will one day come again
to the Land of Israel.

Kristallnacht, November 9, 1938

Aida K. Press

Sudden explosion
in the Jewish Quarter
boots marching
tornado of shattering glass
sidewalks crumbling
minks, Russian sables ripped
from their hangers
O, the fear
O, the wailing
shopkeepers dragged by their beards
children
old men
old women
eye glasses torn from their faces
smashed
bodies beaten to the ground
kicked
trampled
Tod den Juden! *
Tod den Juden!

I am 12 years old
I am there
I am not there
I am across the ocean
at the Metropolitan Theater
in Boston, Massachusetts
watching it with my mother
on the Pathé News.

Bodies
stacked like yesterday's trash
blood running in the gutters
only the sound of the wind wailing

I still hear you.

Death to the Jews!

Spitting in the Wind

Ann Struthers

Oh, my gray shadows, informers, state spies, you are the salt in my soup, the savor, the flavor. I love living on the sharp edge of danger, and when I go home, say my good-byes, I'll miss your carefully noting the themes of my lectures, hoping I'd say something against the regime, the religion. Re-read your scribbles, write that I said, "Democracy and Old Walt Whitman, Poet of Freedom and Voting." I said it. I admit this American fault. And "Emily Dickinson questioned God's goodness." Did you report this error, witnesses for true religion? Did you write down the wicked quotes from *The Scarlet Letter* where Hawthorne cites the position of powerless women? The girls grin. Here's a harlot made heroine, a serious subversion! They pay you so poorly for all these reports, but you need the money to keep you in ciggies, to buy you a pair of knock-off blue jeans. I hope you keep the text books, underline the words that undermine your lives, and may you find a newer country of the mind. Or if you forget them, dismiss them, sell them, then Emily, Walt, Nathaniel, and I spit in the wind.

Harvesting the Moon

Brad Bennett

The moon is hanging so low this evening
that I worry for it.

I worry that uniformed men with chain saws
will scale tall metal ladders and sever the mothy threads
that hold the moon to the darkness.

I worry that they will confiscate it, harvest it, butcher it
to light up executive boardrooms in tall towers,
to feed the neon drip of commercial signs.

I fear that they will bombard it with atomic particles
to forge new weapons of mass destruction
to use in their next war
against the sun.

Postcard From Here

Brad Bennett

Scrape off the impudent birds
from the branches outside your room.

Deadhead all your window box flowers
before they can grow up and bloom.

Snip one single string to each cello
in the orchestra, each guitar in the band.

Spray graffiti on the museum paintings—
tip all the statues from their stands.

Ax down all your shady trees,
plow under your fields of wheat.

Smear mud on your linen place mats
and blood on your very best sheets.

Please tell your precious children
they may be kidnapped in their sleep.

Our government is always at war
and the people here are sheep.

Working a Tug in the Patapsco, December

(In memoriam: Captain Willie Lewis)

Tony Reevy

Floating cars is
a gutsy job.
You lose an arm,
maybe, unloading.
You fall in, you
lose your life.

The Baltimore lights'll
mock you,
you'll try to swim.

The Bay's cold
in December.
You fall in, you
lose your life.

The water'll close
over you,
you slip down.
Maybe float up later
and they find you.

You got to be
cracked to live
this way.
You fall in, you
lose your life.

Ellis Island Ferry

Tony Reevy

I'm remembering it— bedlam. The
stinking launches, blue-coat
officers like Emperor's men.
Lines, screaming ones
turned away. At the end, railroad
men, more blue-coats, one-way
tickets to the Youngstown mill.

My father's neck, pitted with
deep round burns, told the rest
of the story.

Today, we stand in the ferry's bow,
the waters purr by. I squeeze my
granddaughter's hand, my fingers
a creaking claw. She looks up,
sharp— I'm hurting her. How to
tell about the stench, the massed
people. I was a snip of a thing,
too young to hope.

The gorge of my fear rises
as we step off the boat; the
fear takes my eyes and I turn
from the little one to hide my
old face, now young, a boy
again, dirty, hungry, here.

Something to Shoot For

The gun spit and jerked in his arms and the shot went wide, but Edsel was
as thrilled as if he'd made the metal ring. He'd entered grown-up land
where the power was . . .   —Stephen Wright, *M31: A Family Romance*

Arthur Saltzman

I went to one of the eleven local gun shops in the area, to
see what it was about guns.

Do not mistake me. I am not disdainful of people who
collect guns. I don't think of men who spend hours lovingly disas-
sembling and cleaning their rifles as insecure or as fearing they're
insufficiently phallic when they are too long apart from their
armories. I do not think that they are compensating for any
thwarted prowess at work or in bed. While I am alert to the symbol-
ism when Faye Dunaway's Bonnie Parker fondles the pistol by her
pillow when Warren Beatty's Clyde Barrow leaves her frustrated, I
am not convinced that it applies outside the theater. Yet although I
don't equate rifles with erections, I do appreciate how a gun offers
one more way to be reckoned with, and in a society in which people
often feel invisible or at bay, I have some idea where the ferocity of
the pro-gun bumper stickers comes from.

For my own part, though, aside from the toy guns I grew up
with back when sociology saw fit to leave kids to their own de-
meanors and devices—hell, I had a toy chest chockfull of plastic
ordnance from Mattel— I was raised unarmed. My brother and I
kept the requisite cowboy accoutrements in our basement as all
boys and brothers undoubtedly did in theirs. We also had a Tommy
gun, which shot only sound, a dopplering growl that was closer in
quality to a complaining cat than to any firearm's report. Then there
was our deadliest weapon: a Gatling gun, which fired plastic ammo,
or at least it did in the infrequent event that the thing didn't jam.
But our gunplay was always and only that, with the definite emphasis on "play." And limited play at that. I never practiced in the
mirror a Maverick-slick draw, nor did I dream of shooting straight
and true as Burt Lancaster or Kirk Douglas could in the double-

features my parents abandoned us to on summer Saturday after-
noons. Had it been up to me, my ideal career would have been
spent with the Cubs, not in the marshal's office or the FBI. And any
prayers of mine to become lethal and fast had to do with pitching,
not with picking outlaws off their horses or sniping enemy spies.

Let me testify, too, that not one of my toy guns inflicted any
damage whatsoever, neither physical nor psychological, at either
end of the barrel. Neither my brother nor I grew up to have a gun in
the house, and neither of us has ever considered committing a
violent crime or voting Republican. To my mind, that causal connection has always been a myth. To imagine that gangsters pass their
gats on to their kids like some awful genetic legacy is the stuff of
docu-drama and too glib to believe in completely. To think that
committed paintball players, with their twice-weekly amalgam-
ations of Walter Mitty and Audie Murphy, are likelier than the
general population to be institutionalized for destroying more than
just the laundry does not hold up statistically. To argue that Bugsy
Siegel was given a Baretta instead of a fountain pen as a bar
mitzvah gift and that's what set him on his fatal course is pretty
simplistic and just plain false. Our toy artillery notwithstanding, in
my house there was nothing more substantial than my father's
temper and an ambiguous belief in suburban election to stave off
infiltration into our apartment building. You might have found dirty
pictures tucked deep in a dresser drawer, but never a pistol. Nor did
anyone I knew own a gun, most of my friends' fathers having
surrendered their weapons the moment they'd come ashore after
spending their rounds in Europe or Japan.

Face it: Morton Grove was a geographic refutation of the M-
16; no Nazi threatened the equanimity of anyone ensconced in
Skokie, and no one ever visited Old Orchard Mall for ammunition.
Oh, a couple of buddies had BB guns they'd harass birds with.
Mike Wasserman's older brother did manage to assassinate a
sparrow or two in the maple in front of their apartment building, or
so Mike reported. Keith Banazak used to set up empty bottles and
jars in the alley before his one-man firing squad. He eventually
graduated to his dad's Pabst cans—full ones, because of the luscious

bursts they made when hit, followed by the dark, dramatic bleeding of beer. (Keith liked to pretend they were gut-shot Cong.) At least a few guys I knew must have assaulted windows of half-built housing projects at some point, entertainment always being an elusive commodity in those days. But by and large, Evanston, Skokie, Park Ridge, Wheeling—the entire North Suburban area, in fact—constituted a DMZ for as long as I lived there.

In the so-called heart of the country, however, where more folks can recite the Second Amendment than can name a single poet, I've discovered that nearly everyone seems to be packing some sort of heat. Where I live now, men don't hand down shotguns to their children just for show; they don't plug their rifles just to be hung on the living room wall like antiques from Pier One. We're talking about guns that are functional and at the ready. My neighbors assure me that there is a special bond between father and son that only gunning down game can forge. I do not doubt their civic-mindedness, mind you—these are my neighbors, remember, who leave their garbage each week at the end of the driveway and retrieve their mail the same time I do every day. Still, I can't help wondering whether they have a stronger affiliation with the guy who was just arrested south of town for having an ammo dump in his kitchen than they have with me. For theirs is the Other America, identified by NRA memberships, gun racks in truck cabs, and scraps of successfully downed animal adorning darkly paneled dens. They live in the Other America, where boys are more likely to have been introduced to hunting before junior high school than to have played in Little League. In this Other America, kids can distinguish a revolver's caliber and heft more readily than I could have figured out at their age which subway train took you to Wrigley Field. This is where it isn't unusual to see someone in the grocery line or at the gas pump who has a gun stuffed in his waistband or poking partway out of his pocket like an extra genital. To be sure, in this part of the republic, more children have fired weapons than have *taken* trains. (Did I mention that my phone book lists eleven gun dealers in Joplin alone?) Depending on my audience, my confessing in this Other America to never having fired a gun in my life casts doubt upon my parentage, my patriotism, and my sperm count.

Or to be accurate, where I was raised was the Other America, if in definition the majority rules. Growing up in Chicago, the city that featured the ascendancy of Al Capone, I should know as much. (When on vacation in Italy, Cub legend Ernie Banks told a waiter he was from Chicago, the man beamed with recognition: "Ah, Chicago! Bang, bang, eh?" Banks' Hall of Fame credentials could not guarantee the renown that his tenuous connection with a killer did.) Here in southwest Missouri, I am far enough from an urban center that the boundary between military and paramilitary thins, and the term "background check" always inspires someone within earshot to spit. I've learned that in the Show-Me State, often as not, it's your artillery you'll be asked to display. Furthermore, a half-hour's drive south puts me in Arkansas, the Natural State, where, notwithstanding Rousseau, the state of nature is an armed camp. You can buy bullets in any grocery store. Don't be distracted by the cookware and the clothing: for a sizable percentage of its clientele, Wal-Mart is primarily a munitions dump. A straw poll of my students reveals that a militia could be mustered in ten minutes flat because, by my count, pretty much everybody can lay hands on at least one piece apiece.

In short, a far greater percentage of the local citizenry prove their legitimacy by being able to dismantle and load firearms than by producing their Phi Beta Kappa keys, which, to tell the truth, never opened any door anyway. Unless the artist or philosopher I mean to extol had earned a passing score on a target range, or, better yet, shot his way through a thicket or foreign soil, well, save it for the classroom, Professor. Truly, I have no answer to the contention that had Shakespeare the means to arm his heroes properly, his tragedies might have come to better ends. Imagine how much faster—and, frankly, with no greater bloodshed—Hamlet could have expedited his vengeance with a .44 Magnum than he managed to do with all his brooding. "I have seen the day, with my good biting falchion / I would have made them skip," claims Lear, who with a semi-automatic weapon at the ready might have regained both his virility and his throne.

Weaponry is so directed, so purposeful, in a way that poems, with their vague aims and circumlocutions, never are or pretend to be. In *The Shootist* , John Wayne, in the role of aged gunman John Bernard Books, spells out the secret of his longevity: "I've found most people aren't willing. They bat an eye. They hesitate. I won't." Pausing and flinching, edging and inching—the Duke's disdained "other guy" sounds like everybody I went to graduate school with. It also applies to the nature of the novels and poems we focused on. Surely, there is no chance that my reference to Wallace Stevens a couple of sentences ago would have resonated with even one of the absolutely resolute characters John Wayne ever played.

However, even the so-called elevated literature I have always preferred, where most of the action is grammatical and takes place between the ears, and whose movie versions would never tempt a Schwarzenegger or Stallone to sign on to the project, occasionally attest to the appeal of automatic weapons. In particular I think of a moment in Don DeLillo's novel *White Noise* when, at his father-in-law's insistence, a previously pretty feckless professor accepts the gift of a 25-caliber Zumwalt. As a result, he enjoys a visceral impact—a power surge—that no successful class or convention paper could conceivably match."There was something unreal about the experience of holding a gun," he thinks, the paradox being that he confronts the life force more immediately than ever before by handling a deadly weapon. In contrast to the ambient static, in which meanings are illegible and sensations fleeting, the gun seems to root him to something solid and non-negotiable. "How quickly it worked a change in me, numbing my hand even as I sat staring at the thing, not wishing to give it a name." That is the gun's secret genius; it travels through the hand, imparting consequence. Evidently, there is something estimable about a gun, something inherently transitive in a way that no instrument I ever wield can be. It is an instrument of clarity that has nothing in common with the ambiguous means and materials a literature professor employs. Something there is about a gun that wants it discharged. With this in mind, I decided to sneak out of the nook of liberal naiveté, out of my cranny of tenured pacifism, and find out for myself.

As gun shops go, Brandon's Gun Trading Company is comparatively upscale. It appears to cater more to the weapons aficionado and the gun connoisseur than to thrill-seeking teens or vengeful relatives (not that the latter would be easily discerned or denied admittance). There are glossy magazines detailing the latest in high-performance firearms and featuring advice columns with titles like "Views from the Bunker," "The Shooting Gallery," or "Setting My Sights," in which readers endorse or dispute recent refinements made on their favorite guns. There are price guides and brochures, thicker and more explicit than anything you'd find at a car dealership. (I flipped through the Ruger Catalogue of Fine Firearms, whose lavish descriptions and close-up photography of this year's auto-loading rifles, rimfire pistols, and double-action revolvers recalled the quality and content of architectural digests, science journals, and top-shelf porn.) There are displays of cunning mounts and plush holsters for the discriminating shooter. There are a dozen or so gun cabinets, some of them polished steel, some hand-carved oak, richly inlaid, their glass fronts frosted and etched with wilderness scenery. There are long counters featuring intricate new ammunition, all "quality-cast," whose subtle advances you'd need a jeweler's loupe to do justice to. Brandon's is like a gun boutique, really, including lighter, especially fetching pieces for the ladies, as well as starter pistols for the kids. Racks of rifles to riffle through like designer dresses. Every stock gleaming in the fluorescent light. Every barrel oiled bright.

Nevertheless, I couldn't help feeling intimidated by the artillery, as if I'd strayed into enemy territory and unable to affect the foreign accent convincingly enough to pass, here where a wood-burned sign advised ALL VISITORS ENTER AT OWN RISK. I moved self-consciously among the Magnums, Lugers, and Glocks, muttering the guns' guttural names, thuggish things for all their precisely machined reputations, words loaded with grunts. Although I had no plans to fire a weapon that day, I found myself involuntarily bracing for recoil. At the register, the owner (Brandon himself, I presumed) carried on a chummy conversation with a couple of regulars (another presumption) about rumored changes in local permit laws and whether the stopping power of the slimmed-down Glock 36, which one of them was looking at for Father's Day, holds up. A spread of black ammo clips, designed to tantalize, spooked me; they made me think of the joints of some prehistoric predator. Tactical scopes and speed loaders positively seethed with danger. Bullets glinted wickedly on beds of felt.

"Expecting trouble?" I said. My humor tends to grow more pointless and obscure the more nervous I become. Maybe a Glock would settle me down.

Brandon—"The Friendly Expert," as advertised—waved me over. It was stifling in there—no open window or air-conditioning, not even a fan to stir the air—and his golf shirt was black beneath the pits, where twin Ohios of sweat had already formed before noon. Next to the register was propped a photograph of the Brandon women, his wife and three daughters, smiling intensely and looking milk-fed and secure, posed in crinoline and Christian commitment to one another's welfare. It was easy to envision the Brandon clan sitting around the living room together swabbing out the family arsenal the way other families play Monopoly. The wall behind Brandon was plastered with Xeroxes of truculent anti-liberal editorials from the *The Globe*. Also patriotic cartoons and bumper stickers with sayings like SELF-CONTROL, NOT GUN CONTROL and THE SECOND AMENDMENT IS PART OF <u>MY</u> CONSTITUTION. Taped above the rest was a caricature of Hitler giving a Nazi salute, with the caption "All in favor of gun control, raise your right hand."

"You teach out at Southern, don't you?" A tip to urbanites used to the impunity afforded by metropolitan living: apart from decent deli food and jazz, the hardest commodity to come by in the hinterlands is anonymity.

"Right. English."

"English. Uh-huh. I thought I recognized you. So, listen, do you have a wife? Kids?"

"I have a girlfriend. I have a daughter."

"So we're talking loved ones, right? Well, the next time you're out of town and someone decides to break into the house, you tell your girlfriend how much safer she should feel *without* the means to protect herself. Or when some pervert stalks your daughter on her way home from band practice, you tell her not to worry because Mom or Dad *doesn't* have the means to deal with it if the situation escalates."

"Obviously," I answer, risking a defense of my impractical lifestyle, "if you come home to find someone about to kill your family, emotion is going to take over. You're talking burglars and perverts, and in those cases, sure, whose first reaction *wouldn't* be to shoot? But I don't know that I want to *live* that way, anticipating the worst. I just don't think that my case warrants owning a gun, is all."

"Uh-huh. Tell me something, Professor, do they get the newspaper in your part of town? Do we live in the same world, or what?"

This wasn't the first time that someone had questioned my sense of reality and found it oblique at best. You spend twenty or thirty uninterrupted years in the classroom, you live your life in bookish isolation from the repercussive and the tangible, and condescension just goes with the territory. However, I did take Brandon's meaning: if I truly meant to understand anything about guns, I would have to take my education beyond the hypothetical realm where I typically hid out.

Wyandotte, Oklahoma, is so nondescript that the odds are I'd have missed it without the help of the printout I'd made off of MapQuest. It's just one exit off of Highway 60, and taking the bend too fast after Seneca, I had to double back. So far as I knew, Wyandotte's single claim to fame, even among the locals, is that it is the home of the Firing Line. Reportedly, marksmen come from miles around to compete in the regional tournaments the Firing Line sponsors, and, indeed, I wonder if gunnery is the only reason to go to Wyandotte at all. I came on a Tuesday afternoon when I figured it would be relatively cleared out and quiet, figuring that there was no need to embarrass myself in front of more people than I could avoid doing.

The Firing Line looked like a converted warehouse—barely converted, at that. Most impressive was the sheer square footage of the place: a combination sales area, instructional center, and firing range, it stretched further back than the average bowling alley. I was also struck by how gloomy it was—not the drear of Poe or the precipitant dark of film noir so much as the greasy gray of an auto body shop. As opposed to Brandon's emporium, the Firing Line suggested the grimier end of the gun enterprise. The effect there was sparer and less wholesome, and, with the exception of motivational paper targets sporting pictures of Osama bin Laden, Saddam Hussein, and Moamar Kaddafi, less given to winsomeness. If Brandon's was designed to put the customer at ease, the Firing Line was designed to put him on guard. In this context, even the warning sign on the pop machine telling the buyer to be careful when opening cans struck me as ominous.

The proprietor was chatting at the far end of the sales area with a couple of regulars. I started toward them, moving warily past bins of bullets and rifle arrays. I did not interrupt the men but waited quietly until there was a break in the conversation. This wasn't reverence on my part but tentativeness. There was no advantage in pretending to knowledge I didn't have, and I was worried about profaning the place the way American tourists, loaded down with flash cameras and their own cultural baggage, are wont to do in European cathedrals.

"What can I do for you today?"

"I've never fired a gun. I'd like to. Can you help me out?"

By the reaction of all three men, I could see that I had immediately shown myself to be one of a category of patrons, small but predictable, whom they'd sized up as fantasy campers. Some guys with enough disposable income reacted to their mid-life crises by purchasing a workout with the Los Angeles Dodgers; others went skydiving. My bent was cops and robbers. I let them assume. Frankly, I couldn't have explained the day to my friends either. Years ago my divorce stunned many of them, yet I guarantee you that nothing extra-marital I'd done would have struck them as being more out of character for me than my pilgrimage to Wyandotte to open fire.

For the next twenty minutes, while his pals drifted off to inspect some of the more advanced ordnance, Phil, the fellow in charge, instructed me on the capacities and perils of several different handguns. For my maiden shoot, we settled on a .22 and a $25 price for his time and a box of one hundred and twenty rounds.

A couple and their eleven-year-old son came in to buy, so Phil excused himself to run down criteria for them. "Whether you're purchasing something for home defense or a carry gun,"he began, "you want something that you're not gonna be more afraid of than the guy you're pointing it at, am I right? I tell all my customers, too, that if it's a gun you're gonna depend on to save your life, spend some money. The better weapons aren't cheap, but they won't just make the guy you hit mad or suffer. The function of a gun is to protect your loved ones, isn't it? And when you're out of the house, Dad, they're gonna want something they can handle. I mean your boy, too. And whatever you end up getting, get familiar with your gun. I'd say once a week go out and empty a cylinder. Put a mag through it occasionally to keep it and you in tune. So look a few of these over, and I'll be right back with you."

While eavesdropping, I was practicing my lessons on preparing and dismantling my weapon. And how to be sure the safety's on, how to be sure the chamber's empty, how to rest your finger outside the trigger assembly before you're ready to fire, how to rest the gun on the counter after discharging it: I said these precautions under my breath as I did them, much as one murmured during a seder service. On the counter before me was the translucent box of ten dozen bullets, noses up. Expectant, it seemed to me.

"Ready to do some shooting?" Phil gave me glasses and headphones. "The safety glasses are up to you, but you'll need the muffs, believe me." Unquestionably, I thought as we passed through the two sets of double doors to the firing range, I was moving into a new climate. It made sense that he had me dress for it.

He set me up at my booth and, flipping a toggle switch at

my left, brought a backboard abruptly toward us on its pulley. He stapled a large paper sheet to it, then sent it back to a distance of about twenty-five feet. Once more he reviewed the process, making me copy each action to ensure that I was using the right fingers to accomplish it. Pianists begin like this, I thought. Surgeons, too.

"The middle finger presses the cartridge release, remember. The ammo box has a slide top, so you can spill out exactly ten bullets at a time into your right palm, and that's the hand that fills the magazine. Pinch the spring with your left index finger and thumb as you hold the magazine against the table, then force it down. Slot the bullets in back first, one at a time, like that, right hand, right. Once that's done, smack it back in the handle. Go ahead, harder, it can't go off, there's nothing to fire yet." And so on, methodically, trying to deliver the rhythm into my hands. "After half a box or so, you should have already developed some muscle memory. Eventually it'll all seem natural."

Lastly, he closed his hands over mine and showed me how to place my left hand beneath my right to steady it. Even without firing I sensed a shudder: potential energy, perhaps, or the gun's own pulse.

"That way, when the gun jumps, it jumps up, not to the side. You know how they say, 'Don't jump the gun'? Well, in this case, the gun does the jumping. That's how you can remember it. All right? Keep the gun far from your body. Arms locked and out. The straighter you stand, the straighter you'll shoot. Safety off? Okay, whenever you're ready."

The gun barked and snapped in my hands, and it was as if both of us, gun and gunman, were startled by the eruption. I felt less like a soldier or a secret agent than like someone who'd accidentally stepped on a dog's tail.

"The faster you fire—pop, pop, pop—the tighter your spread will be," he called, having to penetrate the headphones. "Go ahead, squeeze 'em off."

And so I did. When Phil was satisfied that I wasn't going to kill anyone or ruin his insurance, he left me for the family of three, who had ventured in with the .38 they'd selected. As he had them take turns practicing filling its cylinders—round rounds into round holes, a psychological test for toddlers—I blasted away, adding spent shells ten at a time to the huge pool of them like a crowded koi pond below me. Sometimes the shells bounced toward my cheek or trickled over and nibbled at my arms, but as I grew easier with the procedure (if not more expert), I was able to ignore them and the odor of burning that increased with each clip I emptied. And I could tell that I was starting to corral my scatter, shot-wise, into a reasonable facsimile of aiming. I was, in the broadest sense of the term, homing in. But I never surrendered to adrenaline, at least not to the extent that I stopped repeating the stations of the gun as I performed them. I made sure I heard that last whispered click denoting a finished clip before relaxing my stance.

Phil slipped in between fusillades. "I've been watching you. You've been tightening your radius all right." He flipped the switch, and the target squealed close. "There. See? Here's where you were earlier," he said, indicating six or seven holes, "and here's the last few groupings." He traced a more compact constellation. "Folks talk about 'gun control'? This is what 'gun control' *really* means. This is the control that *counts* for something. It'll come with practice. You get a discount for ten visits."

Once I exhausted my allotted shots, I toggled the target over to detach it from the board. Only then did I realize that Phil had stapled it on backwards. The concealed front featured a human silhouette—clearly a broad-shouldered male and, despite its lack of features, rather menacing. Concentric rings rippled outward from the center of his chest. To my credit, I suppose, and certainly to my surprise, most of my shots scored; a few even struck the X'd heart.

I did not ask Phil why he'd reversed the target for me. Maybe he had marked me as a vacationing liberal who'd have been inhibited by the sight of a human figure and winced while firing, leading to more collateral than concentrated damage, plus an unimpressive point total. After all, the Firing Line wanted to give even novices like me the incentive to return.

Whatever the logic, I had the perforated figure of an imaginary intruder to take home as a reminder of what I was capable of, and woe to those who'd under-estimate me. The sheet looked like an oversized roll for a player piano, and I considered tacking it to my front door: it would filter the breeze, filling the neighborhood with a song of my prowess and my expanded personality.

Undressing for bed, I wondered what the reaction of my beloved was going to be to this unprecedented aspect of me. Confusion? Amusement? Arousal? It was when I took off my shirt that I found a second souvenir: a shell casing, which must have leapt into my pocket in the midst of one of my barrages. I decided against offering it to her as something to remember me by. My thinking was that since it wasn't representative of the man she knew, it was unlikely that she could remember me by it. On the other hand, throwing it away was out of the question.

I ended up setting it on a bookshelf, in front of the Hemingway. For the time being, anyway, it seems like a decent compromise.

Irony

Elizabeth Swados

Irony actually
Means Iron Knee
Of which there are
Several definitions
One is to have
A knee forged from iron.
To slap it when laughing
And stub the thumb during contact.
Pain and laughter.
Irony

Another definition
Brings to mind
The Native American population.
If for instance
That
Historic plain
Had been named
Iron knee instead of
Wounded Knee
Chances are the earth
Would be too hard
For burials.
And you and I would be
Back in England
Drinking wounded tea.
Irony

And third on this
Decomposition of
The American tongue
Is the definition of

Irony that shouts
Like an inarticulate order.
A man walks into
His penthouse apartment on East 67th Street
It is 1 A.M.
And his knee is conspicuously
Covered in wrinkles and folds
And swollen veins.
Betrayal is everywhere
On the white rug
And the eggshell couch.
His knee is an egg
Half-broken
Dripping
His wife can't
Confront him
Another time…
She just
Wants
A cover up
So she can
Deny
What she's
Always known.
She leaves out the
Predicate and goes at him
"Iron knee" she
screams
"Iron knee before
Someone sees"
Irony!

Deconstructing the Picture

Diane E. Dees

There's Matthew tied to a fence.
Notice the pallor of his waxy skin,
How it accentuates the deep crimson
Splattered across the canvas.
The bruises and lacerations
look so real, the limp body
so close to death, but not quite there.
That's James Byrd on the road,
blood the color of jasper,
his head rolling on the shoulder.
Take note of the white space
surrounding Abner Louima;
there is no grieving crowd.
Brandon's eyes are soft and dry,
his shattered body frail and small,
like the bodies of Carole,
Denise, Cynthia and Addie May
in their just-pressed Sunday dresses—
you can see them there,
under the stained glass, where
the face of Jesus used to be.
Those other children, the very little ones,
hide beneath the empty chairs.
See how the chairs appear to float,
how well illusion is used
to portray evil intentions.
Touch the canvas if you want;
get close, observe the density of color,
the dissonance of context, the irony.
Better still—step back and look
at the big picture: It has almost everything
except a bearded man in sandals in a cave.

A Doctor's Two Days a Week at the Clinic

John Grey

He soaks the blue hairs
just so he can tend the poor.
His bedside manner
stretches from four-poster
to doorway after dark.
For every mansion cough,
there's a down at heel diphtheria.
Each lobster indigestion
pays for a hundred iron-deficient.
His regular practice
overheats credit cards.
The clinic cools down to
whatever empty pockets can provide.
For his attention,
pearls and ermine
vie with old tattoo and ragged coat.
But in his Hippocratic dreams,
placebos waltz with penicillin,
scratches beg at the pit of wounds,
the hungry ride off in their limos,
the smug wait shivering for the bus.

Forgetting by Heart

Steve Schild

Less than two weeks after he'd nailed it
for credit in class,
my fair-haired fourteen-year-old couldn't
recall all of "In Flanders Fields,"
forgetting, at second stanza's start,
"We are the dead." Prodded,
he nodded remembrance that "short days ago/
we lived," and made it on his own
a couple of lines down until
he stumbled again, over
"Take up our quarrel with the foe"
and then there was vague recollection
of breaking faith with those who died
and something about a torch held high
and then, by rhythm more than recognition, he knew
"We shall not sleep, though poppies grow in Flanders
    Fields."

The old man went easy on him
for forgetting, never betting that the rest of us,
older, more in touch with such things,
would ever prove better at remembering
than the boy at the center
of this cold, deadly thing.

All the Saints Are Missing

Arthur Slate

Fiacre is buried under four feet of snow.
Christopher has come unglued
and laying somewhere in the rubble
of coffee cups and cigarette packs.
All of the birds have flown south for the winter
so Francis stands empty-handed,
feeding only air.
With the hawks outpacing the doves
and the olives dying on the branches
Jude will be busy elsewhere.
Tonight there is a halo around the moon,
but all the saints are missing.

By Any Other Name

John N. Miller

Please, doc. I need your diagnosis—
something more medical than *bleeding heart*
my boss and all his sidekicks sneer at.
I know *compassionate conservative*
sounds better, but that's not my problem.
Here. Press your stethoscope against my chest.
Listen to those abnormalities.
Murmurs. Savage thumpings. A clear case
of *hypercardiac proclivity.*
What? Nothing wrong? How can you prescribe
for *Gulf War syndrome, work-related stress,*
malnutrition or *obesity*
and write me off as some health-conscious crank?
Your other patients, doc—
you have the names of their diseases,
you give their suffering a history,
a shared, official-sounding explanation.
You trying to tell me that I want a phony
membership card for their club?
I'm telling you there's something wrong here.
Maybe you're numbed by overwork,
overpay, and high insurance costs.
My heart keeps sending me its troubled message.
Can't you hear it?

Old Opium in a New Sniffer— or a Cynic's Gossip

Louie Crew

My silly fairy friend kept the 11 p.m. Vigil
with his Cardex, like a prayer wheel,
mumbling over the names of 435 "holy" queers
and 37 of their chapters,
while 17 candles flickered before a plaster Mary
and lace draped the poker-chip host,
as if my friend really believed in Resurrection,
or more preposterous, believed that Jesus,
even if resurrected,
would have anything to do with us.

The Elbow Room

Diane Raptosh

It seemed a room safe enough to ask them all in, each
rectangular place at the table shining like lake edge, spaces
between seats wide as forgiveness: Mother and Father, sister
and brother, uncles and aunts, grandparents and great-.
Nobody was dead, no one not speaking, nobody's parts
missing. Their faces turned sunflower: Tiger moths clicked
round our heads. I poured milk for everyone's coffee; it
formed into thumbprints, into ram horns, into small Milky
Ways. Elbows would rise and fall, often in unison. As people
sipped their lips squirmed.

III

DISSONANCE

Coat of Many Colors

Barry Ballard

The woman on the corner has fallen
asleep, as the rest of us briskly walk
by or drive around her situation.
She is almost hidden in her thick wool
coat that has become a room in a condemned
building that protects her from the sharp squawk
of tame crows, or the boiling invasion
of gases from the underground drainage pools.

It is obviously a coat of wished
colors, although I can only see the half
that's gray and its fraying collar, a spun
gift from a god that doesn't seem to exist,
a god who will find it later, stained, and ask,
"Where is my daughter? What have you done?"

Peace

Barry Ballard

If Yeats was right and "peace drips from the veil
of morning," then I wonder how he'd see
the mother and child resting on the bench under
the failing streetlight, blinking on and off. How
do they fit when peace is strangled in the pale
mist of carbon-monoxide, or defeated
like wild birds that barely fly? What hurt
has altered what they're made of, or allowed

us only the half-miracle of seeing
them in life's vaporous flickering fog?
We can only imagine the unconnected
side of our intersecting lives: being
the improbable friend, the childhood never fed,
the outstretched arm when the world drives off.

Moral Development

Sally Allen McNall

I was eight when Mary Ann,
my best friend, told me about the beatings.
I think now there was more to tell
she didn't yet have words for.
My whole body was suddenly
strung and twitching with conviction—
the awful wrong, the need to right it.

I look at us now from fifty years on,
two skinny girls in their cotton school dresses,
knobby-kneed, smart-mouthed.
I see her tears slide slowly
from under her sparkly
cat's-eye glasses and I feel again raw pity.
Her split lip, her head bent
so I looked at the clumsy part of her hair, her hands
making wrinkles in her starched skirt,
and the flood of her shame, and my blood coursing
black under ice toward justice.
I went to my parents with Mary Ann's story.
I went to my mother and father, demanding justice,
demanding they save my friend.

I remember the storm of my disappointment,
what it smashed, what it blew away.
With my smart mouth, then, I questioned
their bravery, their goodness.
When my father pulled down my underpants
to spank me, the rule was *I stop when you cry*.
I was one day closer to the day
I would refuse to cry.

I think of all the world's daughters who cry
or refuse to cry, in dangerous places
in our dangerous time.
It rises up in me again,
my icy, forlorn pride.

I get it

Sally Allen McNall

at the end of the cereal aisle the girl
fourteen maybe fifteen stands sideways

face a few inches from the packages of oatmeal
and says I'm sorry I'm sorry I'm sorry

I slide my cart past her thinking what to do
and see her mother, the same hair, bones

of their faces glistening through wrenched
skin, and the man whose skin

is full of blood, whose eyes are so wide
I see the crazy rim of white above the iris

he allows the woman to hold him by one
dense vibrating arm, hold him back

from the girl while he says she never gets
it, she never gets it, she never gets it

and I keep going, I don't even catch
the eye of any other shoppers

I don't know why they keep going
I know why I do

The Gwitch'in Girl's Family Tree

Kenneth Rehill

In an hour interview,
the social worker had crossed out
more lines than she'd left intact.
Now Betty would clear up
all the confusion.
"Auntie Amy is actually
my second cousin
on my mother's side,
but I lived with her
for two years, until I was nine.
Two uncles are unrelated except
they always hunt with my father.
My brother, Fred, is my brother.
But Brother Chad just lived
with us when he was a lad.
Grandpa Paul came from Idaho
ten years ago and isn't Gwitch'in.
He fishes with Fred and gives
moose meat to Grandmother Mary,
who is my mother's cousin."
The interviewer sat
with pen poised and brow knitted.
She'd need fresh forms.

For Dru and Katie
and All the Girls Who Disappear
Kirsten Dierking

At recess once I was playing tag,
running away from the other kids,
when I opened my eyes, I was
lying face down in a far corner
of the empty schoolyard, I never
really knew what happened,

how easily the continuous thread
of our lives can be broken. The
missing pieces we never get back.
The things we take to our last moment,
not knowing, not ever understood.

The Cut Girls

Elizabeth Levitski

Promised gifts
and told to be brave
they are led
in the sanctified name of tradition
like sheep
   to slaughter,
the cold river water in which
they are made to sit,
    not cold enough
to numb the pain.

I do not want to think of
the blunt edge
   of the penknife,
the shard of
broken glass,
the tin lid, the razor blade;
not of the blindfolds,
the rags
they stuff
   in their mouths
to silence their screams,
how they hold them down,
how they spread
their legs.
   It's too much, the reasons they give -
that it's ugly, a danger
to men. But when
my body sings
its thunder beneath
the tender tongue
   of love

I feel them shiver
in the garden
of my conscience, pleasureless
and ignorant,
aching like lilies
           to bloom.

Truce

Allison Whittenberg

For the girl abused by her father,
The terrible is the beautiful

In between, he showed range
Embracing a new word from the family dictionary:
Fun

A pumpkin nearly half her size that he let her pick
They came home from the patch and clawed out its guts

He put the face in the window

Without a recipe, they baked happiness on the stunted, grey
  afternoon
A can of condensed milk and molasses

The outside, cold as reality
Inside, warm, warm as television

They laughed when the pie turned out to be a horrid tasting
  neon orange mess
Because that day, they were not tragic figures;
They were horrible cooks.

Prayer in the Schools

Merna Ann Hecht

As if the classroom windows had flown open
as if flocks of swallows came in
changing darts of the mind's directions.
As if worn out languages like measurement or government
    flew out the window
and a prayed for tenderness beyond what we could know
alighted between us.

All we did was push back the desks,
out came baskets, boxes, clothes trees,
hats, velvets, wigs, capes, moustaches, hoop underskirts,
topcoats. The teacher's desk crowded
with old age kits, clown white, vials of silver and glitter,
pots of rouge, lip and face liners, powders and shadows.

Quicker than swallows plume and dive
the children readied themselves,
costumes completed,
they presented us their faces.

As if our fingers rouged and brightened the moment itself,
touched a delicacy of time as to take it apart, slow it down,
we rubbed our fingertips on the jawline of a trust so complete
we could never speak of it. Closer than air between us
came a tenderness, fingers layered on soft cheeks
traced bone structure back to childhood.

> *Say a prayer for innocence of uplifted faces,*
> *for time stilled with wingbrush,*
> *time when no child will be left*
> *behind razor wire, seized borders, starved and frail*
> *in arms of weeping mothers*
> *on all sides of he sea.*

Pray for open windows across the world's school room,
surprise swallows with imagination's wings,
to fly the children in and out of lines
of the world
they teach us to trust.

Maiden's Prayer

R. Yurman

Stretch my neck until it's stately.
Stretch my lips 'till I can't speak

Tie knots in my hair that it not grow wild.
Sew knots in my intestines so I won't eat.

Stitch my bedclothes tight around me.
Stitch my labia that I stay chaste.

Paralyze my thighs to prevent my running
Tether my voice to keep my singing tame.

Possess my all too lively spirit.
Control my visions and my tastes.

Hobble my brain so my thoughts must shuffle.
Hobble my feet that I may not leave.
Shut the school doors in my face.

Cinch my waist to keep my figure trim.
Veil my eyes that no one else may see them.
Drape my limbs that I not tempt men.

May these cuts and bruises
fill me with no terror,
when, knees pressed together,
pulse a maddened flutter,
I evade your power
in my rich and deep disguise.

Dissonant Concerto

Shirley A. Powers

Perhaps it's in the tuning
of the piano, the perfect fifths
slightly augmented or diminished.
The off tune chords caused by
the way the earth wobbled on its axis,
shifting the North Pole one inch,
shrinking the day's length
three millionths of a second,
leaving tsunami twisted trees and
lifeless bodies on distant shores.

The dissonance might be caused by
ocean temperatures rising as glaciers melt.
Smoke from the ruins of Fallujah
might carry the answer
Ruins, where a young man weeps over finding
his small sister's doll, one leg
and one eye missing.
Perhaps the discordance results from
sequestering the Goddess in the
pages of history
heeding only the God of vengeance.

Circle

Julie Herrick White

I will never preach
from this pulpit again,
the preacher said,
because it has been defiled
by a woman.

Women are great defilers
with their homemade soup
and laundry and soapsuds
and husbands home late
and dishes that crack unexpectedly.

Women are great defilers,
and in India, they are
sometimes covered with kerosene
and burned to death.

Her dress caught on fire, they say.
Flames out of control.
A kitchen accident.

A woman out of control, they say.
Marriage and trepidation.
Children with fevers rising.
Husbands home late.
Dishes cracked. Pulpits defiled.

Wordsworth Hears of the Death of Robespierre

Robert Cooperman

I was walking in the Sca Fells,
iron clouds and bright sun
alternating as if the shadows
of a blade were falling and rising
along the crags, when of a sudden
Dorothy ran toward me,
her skirts wild as the sky;
she waved a newspaper
like a flag of freedom.

I read, the news like fireworks
in my head; we invented a jig of joy,
hurrahed, "Good riddance
to the bloodthirsty tyrant!"
as if the cleverest measures
I'd ever composed.

Then I stopped, remembered
Annette and our daughter in France,
and my promise to return to them
broken by ten years of war.
The Channel crossing not nearly
so storm-tossed as the woman
who would now have to be told
of my new, English, suitable love:
delightful and wise Mary Hutchinson,

I grasped dear Dorothy's hand;
my sister would gladly volunteer
to undertake this obligation
were I to murmur one word of it,
which I must not,
though she's already guessed.

Gauntlet

Laura Gibson

I ran
the gauntlet
of the human life chain
today.

Jesus Forgives and Heals

A solid two miles of them,
standing on the curb,
fanned up and over the hill
in my town.

Pray to End Abortion

Old and young
held signs,
making eye contact
with passengers of cars
swimming against them.

Stop Abortion Now

And marching up and down the line
with a clipboard and a black overcoat
strode a girl, much younger than me.
Her nametag read: *LifeLine Marshall*.
Erecting troops for this holy war,
she sailed on conviction and responsibility
at what her organization had reaped, a
solid statement of morality.

Abortion Hurts Women

Dipping their toes into the
mainstream of traffic,
a group of girls smiled
and waved
their placards
my way.

Equal Rights for Unborn Women

I wanted to call out to these little girls
looking for approval from elders and
flaunting adult messages.
The future for them will not be
black and white like
stark signs they hold in front
of their nubile chests.

Abortion Kills Children

Not old enough to vote,
they are the new soldiers,
the fay messengers
of pedants and hate-mongers.

God Hates Killing

My right turn lay just
beyond the end of the line.
Midriffs bare, two teenage girls
shared the duty of the parting message.

Pray, sinners, for the life within you

Ida B. Wells: Letter to My Children's Children

Wilda Morris

I was born in slavery,
but when I was twenty-five
I refused to give up
my seat in the lady's car
on the Chesapeake & Ohio
to a white man.
The conductor and baggagemen
dragged me off the train
as other passengers cheered.
I sued and won my case
but the ruling was overturned
by the Tennessee Supreme Court.

My friends Calvin McDowell,
Thomas Moss and Henry Stewart
were arrested for defending
their grocery store against attack,
jailed, then lynched. I couldn't stand
the thought of three fine men
hung from the branches of a tree.
I wrote my rage. A mob destroyed
the office of the *Free Speech and Highlight.*

Don't tell me you had a tough start
in life, that you're too young
to make a difference. Just get started.

The News

Wilda Morris

That day I saw the same news
as everyone else,
helicopter down, soldiers dead,

bombs dropped on Baghdad.
tanks exploding, prisoners of war,
a child with bloody bandaged head.

When the phone rang,
I heard your news,
mail box knocked down,

rocks thrown at your windows,
your scarfed daughter cursed.
It's never only *over there*

when hate is loosed
and violence strikes
like lightning across the globe.

I'd stand between you
and the storm
if I knew how.

Resurrection

Wilda Morris

The Prince of Peace must have wept
seeing the Nitrian monks
drag Hypatia to the Caesarian Church
strip her, pummel her with clay tiles,
hack her body into pieces
and burn the ravaged remains.

No more would she don
her philosopher's cloak
gathering lovers of learning
by her eloquence and clarity.

No more would her lips
teach Neo-Platonism.
No more would her pen
write mathematical commentaries.

Her attackers lie nameless
in unknown graves.
Hypatia rises again through the pages
of Descartes, Newton, Leibniz.

The Peace Worker

In memory of Margaret Hassan
d. November, 2004

Aida Press

She came in peace to Iraq
more than 30 years ago
to care for the poor
the ragged and the hungry
especially the children.
She married an Iraqi.
She converted to Islam.
They were her people.
She was one of them.

I see her living face
beaming at me from
the *New York Times*
whole, welcoming, competent
in charge of Care International
in her chosen country.
Even al-Zarqawi pleaded
for her life.

You holy son of Islam
you who shot her
point-blank in the head
are you dancing in the street
are you drunk on forbidden wine
do you slap your thigh with glee
do your comrades pound you on the back
do you touch your forehead to the ground
all in the name of Allah?

Where does it say
in your holy book
thou shalt gun down
the giver of food and drink?
Where does it say
thou shalt kill
the giver of solace
the giver of love?

"Partners in Crime"

John Roman

"It is important to note that a child's primary view of the world
is developed through the relationship the child has with his or her
parents."
Dr. Wayne Kritsberg,
"The Adult Children of Alcoholic Syndrome"
1985

I was thirteen years of age when my father took up drinking again. He'd stopped drinking for about two years and seemed like a completely different person during that time in comparison to the horribly abusive man I had come to know and fear in the very early years of my life. My father's newly found interest in his five sons was not only a pleasant surprise but also a joy to us all. As the oldest boy, I had come to expect the worst from my father, having sampled the unpredictability and ferocity of his moods and temper. My little brothers were too young to have witnessed some of his explosions or to have been on the receiving end of his rage. But during the period of his non-drinking, I slowly learned to trust and admire the man who was my father for the first time in my life.

I noticed a change in him very early in his sobriety. One sunny afternoon during my eleventh summer, my father returned home from work with a huge coil of industrial-type rope and an old, oversized truck tire sticking out of the trunk of his car. He climbed the hill behind our house carrying the rope under one arm and the tire under the other and dropped both at the base of a towering eighty-foot oak tree at the crest of the hill. I watched from indoors as my little brothers ran up the hill with their dad and jumped around at his feet. I could see my father staring up into the tree and planning his strategy to climb it while simultaneously tying one end of the rope around his waist.

My father was halfway up the tree, with the rope uncoiling as he climbed, before my mother even realized he had come home from work. She ran out of the house and screamed at my father from the bottom of the hill at the horror of his being up the tree. Then she ran up the hill toward the tree, her screams persisting every leap of the way. By this time, my curiosity dramatically aroused and my father in a place where he could do me no immediate harm, I too came out of the house and went to the hilltop to join the others.

By the time I got to the tree, my father was way, way up there, the rope on the ground continuing to uncoil as he climbed and climbed. "Be careful!" my mother kept screaming over and over again. My younger brothers squealed with glee at the sight of their father being so high in the tree. I just stood there and stared in awe, surprised at my father's agility and courage. None of us had any idea what he was up to and our collective amazement grew even more intense when my father stopped ascending the tree and began to crawl on his stomach out onto a large, thick limb, which protruded out and over the clearing where we all stood below. By this time a small group of neighbors had also gathered with us at the tree.

About three-quarters of the way out on the limb, he stopped, untied the rope from his waist and began tying it to the section of limb just out in front of him, a good amount of coiled rope was still on the ground despite his height. All of us were silent. He had to be at least sixty feet off the ground. Our necks crooked to watch as he somehow knotted that thick, fibrous rope while maintaining perfect balance on his stomach. The hefty branch he lay on shook, creaked and spewed leaves as he worked. The rope didn't appear to tie easily, but somehow he managed three good knots in it. The rope's length and weight was evident as it sluggishly wiggled with erratic movements out in the open space under him. Then came the frightening part. Once the rope was secured to the limb, my father threw himself off the limb and grabbed onto the rope. Using the rope like a fireman's ladder, but using his hands in a series of successive grabs to slow his descent, he shimmied his way safely back to the ground.

No sooner he hit the ground, he grabbed the remaining

rope lying on the ground, eye-balled a measurement, and quickly cut it with a with an odd-looking curved utility knife, which I hadn't noticed he'd thrown to the ground with the tire and rope. Once cut, he picked up the big truck tire with one hand and tied it to the rope. We were now the proud owners of a tire swing! But not just any tire swing. This one had the longest swinging range I've ever seen on a tire swing before or since, the top of the fulcrum being incredibly high from the ground. As my father cleaned up the leaves and rope remnants around the base of the tree, my brothers were already giving the swing its first test drive, all four of them huddled together in a lump on the truck tire with an occasional foot popping out to kick the ground for more velocity. While they played my father turned to me and, completely out of character, patiently explained how he had tied the knot in the rope with a bit wider opening than the width of the tree limb to allow for the later growth and expansion of that limb. Ten years later that tire swing would still be functional, still be strong.

The tire swing episode turned out to be the first of many marvels my father created for his sons during those mandatory years of sobriety. I say mandatory because the Connecticut Department of Motor Vehicles, knowing the livelihood of our family depended on my father having a license, allowed him to continue driving as long as he refrained from alcohol for a period of two years. This sentence was handed down after my father rolled over our 1956 Chevy Nomad station wagon late one evening on his way home from a typical long night of drinking. But even before his accident, even with the limited consciousness of a child, I always felt his reckless and irresponsible behavior was nothing short of a crime. A crime that no one in the family spoke about. A crime against five very young children who needed a strong, sober and nurturing dad to look up to. The sentence handed down turned out to be a blessing in disguise for my brothers and me. It gave us back our father and introduced us to the man he really was.

I remember another time, a Friday afternoon, when my father came home in the middle of the day driving a big dump truck. The back of the truck was filled with probably over a hundred tree bark boards. These were the long, shaved off parts of tree logs, the middle sections most likely being turned into square beams. These leftover boards were about fourteen inches wide and only about an inch thick. Their lengths ranged anywhere from eight to fifteen feet, their fronts slightly rounded and still containing all the actual tree bark. He dumped the load into a pile at the end of our driveway and returned to work. When he got home later that evening he got right to work with his creation.

With two-by-fours that had been stashed in the basement for years my father started constructing a ten-foot by ten-foot skeleton for a playhouse using a large, live maple tree in the side yard as the corner anchor to the structure. All weekend he sawed, nailed and hammered out the framework, attaching it all to the trunk of the maple. We kids helped as best as we could. He was intense when he worked and I, still not trusting him fully, managed to find peripheral tasks that kept me busy at a safe distance from wherever he happened to be working. What developed by the end of the weekend was a solidly built faux log cabin standing about eight feet off the ground on a slightly raised plywood platform base. It was sheathed on its sides with the boards of tree bark, the boards nailed one above the other to the entire surface of the house gave it the distinct appearance of being a real log cabin. The cabin even had a window and door opening as well as a flat, plywood and tarpaper roof, which was able to support the weight of all five of us at one time. Of course the only way to get to the roof was by climbing the tree. The end result was an artistic, architectural and engineering marvel that was the envy of every kid in the neighborhood.

We were beginning to expect the unexpected from my father, but in a positive sense in contrast to his earlier, explosive drinking days. What I noticed in particular about my father was a new sense of calm and patience, attributes that simply did not exist earlier. Gone were the beatings with the leather belt, the mockery, the belittlement, and the cruel verbal assaults. I was even beginning to feel safe in the same room with him without fear of getting slapped across the back of the head for no other reason than being in his way. Instead, evidence of genuine concern for his sons, outward displays of compassion, and participation in his children's interests were beginning to appear.

Like the time he surprised my brother George, who at age ten was starting to show an interest in ham radios. Father built him a short-wave radio antenna in the back yard by stringing a long metal wire between two large pines. And it worked! Or the time in the dead of winter when he constructed a very low, rectangular retaining wall that encompassed an entire flat area of our yard, then flooded it with the garden hose to create a homemade, yet very effective ice-skating rink for his boys.

Then there was the summer my father conceived of a way for his sons to earn some extra money by catching night-crawler worms. We stored the live worms in our basement in a small refrigerator my dad had picked up cheap from the classifieds. He nailed a tiny wooden, hand-painted sign that simply said "Live Bait," and the fisherman's cars immediately began to arrive! Every sale was an event to my brothers and me. Events out of proportion to the reality of those simple purchases of twenty-five cents or so. For two summers we kept the business thriving, our summer nights spent in ecstasy as we felt we were literally pulling cash out of the ground! It created a bonding and a sense of sharing between the five of us.

Another fond memory of mine happened one early summer evening at the dinner table. Looking out the kitchen window at my bicycle in the yard, I made a passing comment of comical disgust about the sorry state of my bike, it being an assemblage of numerous sections and mis-matched pieces salvaged from older junked bicycles. My father leaned over from his place at the table and peeked out the window at the bike. "You're right," he said. "I never noticed that before." As the dinner ended and the table was being cleared, my father asked me if I'd accompany him while he ran an errand in town. Well, the errand turned out to be a trip to Sears to buy me a brand new, bright red Schwinn three-speed bike that shined like a new car. I still have clear images in my mind of test-driving that bike around the Sears parking lot and being able to see my father's image silhouetted against a large plate glass window as he paid for the bike.

During that short period of my youth, un-planned trips to
the movies and spontaneous nights out for supper became the
norm. Any afternoon my father might walk through the door with
pizzas, ice cream or surprises for us! I'll never forget the day he
came home from work in a pouring, drenching rain lugging a large
box with a blanket over it. He put the box down on the kitchen floor
and watched our reactions as he slowly removed the blanket to
reveal a color television set! The first color television set we'd ever
owned and the very first one in our neighborhood.

He was always bringing home cardboard boxes filled with
paper, drawing supplies and pencils he'd picked up at work. One
evening he returned with a small fruit basket with baby squirrels in
it whose mother had been killed that day by a utility crew, which
we fed and nursed before turning over to a shelter. Another time he
brought us a second-hand 8-millimeter movie projector with several
short cartoon films in it. The night he arrived with a big, black
leather case stands out clearly in my mind. The case opened to
display a reel-to-reel tape recorder. We had hours and hours of fun
playing with that! And I vividly remember the afternoon he unexpectedly came home early carrying a rectangular-shaped paper bag
that he placed down on the kitchen table to the glees and chants of
my little brothers. He slowly opened the top of the bag, put his
hand in it, paused to look at us all, then pulled out a six-pack of
beer.

That was it. The two years were up to the day. That was the
end. I was thirteen and for some odd reason I remember it was a
Wednesday and it was autumn. My little brothers didn't even know
what exactly it was he took out of the bag. They thought it was for
them, soft drinks or something. But I knew. I had memories they
lacked. When my father opened one of the beers and retired to the
living room to watch television, I immediately broke into a hushed
but hostile verbal assault on my mother, careful not to let my father
hear me. "You're going to let him start drinking again?" I quietly
cried once, twice, three times in a panicky whisper. Over and over
again I repeated this sentence, following her around the kitchen,

each time with more emphasis and more alarm. But my mother continued her preparation of the evening meal refusing to acknowledge my questions and pretending not to even recognize my presence in the room. Finally, after my persistence and visible emotional excitement, without looking at me she said in a matter-of-fact tone, "He only needs one beer to help him relax."

Her passive attitude and lack of concern that a return to the old days was a real possibility, made me even more upset. "Sure!" I almost screamed, "One beer tonight, then two tomorrow, and next week he's bombed by eight-o-clock!" For several minutes I was engaged in a confusing, one-sided debate with her. Confusing in that a thirteen-year-old boy should be trying to explain common sense logic to his adult parent. Confusing that it would even be necessary for me to have to enlighten my mother to the dangers of allowing my father to return to his old habits. But all my efforts fell on deaf ears. That was it. That was the end. That was the last day I saw the father that I was just beginning to know, respect and love.

Slowly but certainly more and more alcohol was required each evening to attain the blood-alcohol level necessary "to help him relax." It was not clear to me why my father started drinking again, but it was obvious that alcohol did not agree with him. It took him over. Especially in the consistently large amounts he was consuming every day of the week. Gradually he became less and less enthusiastic for the happiness and spiritual care of his sons. His temper and short fuse made a comeback. Within a few months, the beatings began again with even more severity than before. Harsh whippings with a leather belt that left external and internal wounds on my brothers and me. Forty years later those internal wounds would still be open and unhealed, and would provide the breeding ground for germs of division, disrespect and hostility between the five of us.

For me, all real connection to my father came to an end on an evening when I was fourteen years old. In an attempt to intervene in a violent physical altercation between my mother and father, my father punched me in the head with his fist, dropping me to the dining room floor. I was literally knocked unconscious for several seconds. When I regained consciousness my father was standing over me, both of his legs straddled over my body. Fists clenched and held out in front of him he looked down at me and yelled, "Come on! Get up! You want some more of this you goddamned little bastard? Come on! Get up and fight like a man!" This was the person I would know as my father for the rest of my life and his.

The environment at home became so bad that four years later, just after graduating from high school, I left home for fear of my personal safety. Nowhere to go, I lived on the street for a while before joining the Army. Spiritually, I never really did go back there. My father's alcoholism, violence, disrespect and verbal assaults persisted for decades and I saw its repercussions on the habits, behaviors and personalities of my family as a whole. I always felt my father's return to drinking was nothing short of a crime. A crime that no one in the family spoke about. A crime against five innocent young boys who deserved better, their childhoods lost, their full potentials never to be realized.

Most certainly my father is guilty. But before this case is closed and a sentence is handed down, perhaps it would be wise to investigate further to see if he might have had an accomplice working with him.

August 19, 1999

Lyn Lifshin

It was this day nine
years ago I couldn't
stay awake in the café,
even after 3 cups of
coffee. One hospice
nurse said "3 weeks
for your mother" and
so I was sure I could
manage anything, just
be there, forget to sleep.
We cooked chicken
soup the way she liked
it and watched 3 movies
in her room. She wanted
to help me cut up the
broccoli, no, zucchini.
Steamed and soft, we
ate it on the floor in her
room as she wanted a
taste of this and that
and then talked with 3
or four friends and
relatives. "A good day,"
she grinned as I rubbed
her back at 11 and the
night nurse came in
less than 24 hours before
she wouldn't be needed

Children of Survivors

Lyn Lifshin

When we went to
the museum so many
years later, I sat
them down, asked
them to tell me
what happened
and my mother told
me that long before
the camps it was
cold. There was no
food. Whatever he got,
my father didn't
want to eat, he
saved it for me. I
was old enough to know
I didn't want to take
his bread, wouldn't
take it

I Remember Haifa Being Lovely But
Lyn Lifshin

There were snakes in the
tent my mother was
strong but she never
slept, was afraid of
dreaming. In Auschwitz
there was a numbness,
lull of just staying
alive. Her two babies
gassed before her, Dr.
Mengele you know who
he is? She kept her
young sister alive
only to have her die
in her arms the night
of liberation. My mother
is big boned but she
weighed under 80 lbs.
It was hot, I thought
the snakes lovely. No
drugs in Israel, no
food. I got pneumonia,
my mother knocked the
doctor to the floor
when they refused,
said I lost two in
the camp and if this
one dies I'll kill
myself in front of
you. I thought that
once you became a
mother, blue numbers
appeared mysteriously,
tattooed on your arm.

You Should Throw Out Our Mother's Clothes, Her Combs

Lyn Lifshin

you can't move on,
get on with things
unless you get rid
of what's behind
you a friend says.
But I don't trust
what's ahead, am
someone leaving,
facing away from
where they are
going. Or like
some animal with
eyes at the back of
its head. My neck
aches from trying
to watch what is
dissolving, trans-
formed somehow
in this afternoon
light. My mother,
in this after-life
holds me caught as
Lot's wife, so tight
sometimes I feel
I can't grow

The Moon Jacket

Ruth Latta

Every November, at Aspen Grove School, someone unpacks the costumes of Christmases past to see what can be re-used for this year's concert. The senior room teacher chooses girls from Grade 7 or 8 to sort the garments in the junior room cloakroom.

"Cheryl," says Mr. Flynn. Her family has lived in the area for three generations.

"And Melda." Slumped in her desk, Melda is taken by surprise. She springs to her feet and pulls her cuff over her forearm.

Earlier, when Mr. Flynn asked her who holds the Nobel Peace Prize, she went blank, though she knows that it's the Prime Minister, Mr. Pearson.

Melda has never before attended a country school. Since Grandma's death, she has lived with five different families and attended a different school each year. Here at Aspen Grove, everyone is friendly. Her foster parents, the Mortens, are disappointments, but she must get along, so as not to be moved away from this school.

In the hall, the girls rap on Mrs. Abbott's door. The stout grayhaired woman bustles over to greet them. "Continue reading, Grade 4," she calls over her shoulder.

"'Silver', by Walter de la Mare," reads a boy. *"Softly, silently now, the moon, walks the night in her silver shoon."*

The six year olds are building a village in the sand box. The girls go past to the cloakroom, where cardboard boxes have been taken down from the cupboards, and wait on the floor. Mrs. Abbott tells them to take out anything that might be suitable for this year's program, and put it in the empty box.

As the teacher returns to her class, Cheryl pulls out gauzy pastel cheesecloth dresses once used for a play. Melda gasps at a papier-mâché bull's head, and Cheryl tells her about a number involving toreadors and a dancing bull at a previous concert. The bull's head has flaring pink nostrils that remind Melda of Mr.

Morten's nose. At twelve, she's too old to give goodnight kisses, and she hates his big lips and malodorous breath.

Last night, she escaped to her bedroom, a converted back porch with a warped door which he almost broke down. But his wife shouted for him to "get away from there," and he retreated to the sofa, where he'd fallen asleep.

He was still snoring when Melda got up for school, but Mrs. Morten was up and dressed, though pale. When Melda mentioned that there was no margarine and that the bread was moldy, Mrs. Morton swished her hair back off her face and called her a whiner. "And quit flaunting yourself around Mr. Morten." She seized Melda's arm and dug her fingernails into it, breaking the skin and leaving bruises. Melda left in tears, and has spent the day trying to keep her wrist covered.

Flaunt herself? She moved as quietly as possible.

Two woolly costumes from the "Teddy Bears' Picnic" go into the box to be recycled as sheep in the Nativity Play. Then Melda's hand touches something silky, and she pulls out a beautiful garment of satin. On a blue background shine golden crescent moons and stars. She slips it on. It's much too big, but the fabric makes her feel like a star. The label says, "Milady's Boudoir."

She wishes it were hers. Often, when the wood stove goes out it is cold at the Mortens. She wears her sweater over her night-gown, or goes to bed fully clothed. She may have to sleep in her parka when winter sets in. For the time being, this garment would be wonderful to wear on top of her nightgown.

"Look!" Cheryl holds up a pair of bright red shoes. "From *The Wizard of Oz*."

Melda knows the story. In fact, she has tried clicking her heels together and saying, "There's no place like home," but the magic doesn't work for her.

If another family in this community would take her, she'd abandon the drunken Mortens in a minute, but she doesn't know many people yet. She was invited to Cheryl's for dinner one night, but not to sleep over, as Cheryl's home is full of children.

Melda likes this junior room family with Mrs. Abbott as

mother. The sun is low in the sky, shining through the windows on the golden desks. Mrs. Abbott's dress is a warm brown too. 'If only this moment could be forever,' she wishes, as she folds the blue cloth for Mary's mantle.

Mrs. Abbott returns at 3:15, and smiles at Melda in the star-studded satiny garment. "My old bedjacket," she says. "A gift from my daughters. Too small, now."

As Melda slips out of the garment, Mrs. Abbott sees her arm and exclaims over it.

Melda has a story ready. "I was cleaning up Mortens' yard."

"Oh, dear. Is it painful?"

Melda shakes her head, but today she could hardly write.

"Thanks, girls. You can finish tomorrow. Now, you don't want to miss your bus."

Back in the senior room, Melda puts her reader into her schoolbag. She will lose herself in it back in her porch bedroom, pretending it is homework. Of course, Mrs. Morten may complain that she is wasting electricity and should come out and study at the kitchen table.

Occasionally the Mortens forget that she is there, as they sit in their sprung easy chairs in front of the TV, but sooner or later they always remember her.

Climbing into the bus, she notices a 1952 International Harvester pick-up truck parked behind the custodian's car. A pleasant-looking gray-haired man is behind the wheel. It's Mr Abbott. The other day, out on the Morten's Dogpatch yard picking up beer bottles and paper bags, she saw that truck go past, and it was all she could do not to run after it, calling, "Take me with you."

The Mortens were drunks, but good actors. They must have cleaned up the house and themselves on first applying to take foster kids. No other foster homes had been as bad as theirs, though a couple had come close. In one, she'd shared a bed with a boy who kept poking her with a stick at night. She mentioned this behavior to her social worker and was abruptly moved. In the new place, she'd had to help the mother with both her preschoolers and the ferrets, which she bred for sale. Chasing after a toddler, Melda tripped over the ferrets' cage and they escaped. Next thing she knew, the mother was shouting over the phone to social services.

Next she'd had the good luck to be sent to a kind, stable family. All was well until the father was electrocuted in an accident at work. The mother became a basket case who couldn't cope with her own kids, let alone a foster one. Melda was moved again.

In the next home, she and three other girls her age all slept in bunks in a big room upstairs. It was fun, but soon the foster parents decided that they could make more money boarding college students instead.

Now, as the orange bus lumbers along, Melda looks out the window at the yellow leaves, the color of Mrs. Abbott's favorite dress. Mrs. Abbott resembles Grandma, but Melda knows better than to confuse the two. The teacher's kindliness is a professional attitude. Mrs. Abbott already has two daughters, both at university, and although she claims to miss them, she has also mentioned putting up her quilting frames in Liz's room, and turning Lynn's into an office. The young women's faces gleam out of a gold frame on Mrs. Abbott's desk. The light falls on their hair, creating haloes. Their cheeks are as rosy as the apple that always sits beside them.

"If my parents had lived," Melda muses, "would I be pretty and smart?" They had died in a car accident when she was two.

The bus draws to a stop near the Mortens' mailbox. Thank goodness a row of evergreens hides the house. Melda is embar-rassed by the barn board box house with a sagging veranda and a back porch opening into space.

The car is gone. Are the Mortens at the village laundromat, or at the Watering Hole? They always return sloshed. Meanwhile, she has the place to herself. With difficulty, she makes a fire in the cookstove. She is inexperienced in handling matches and kindling and has a sense of accomplishment when the birch begins to burn. She thinks of lighting the heater stove, then thinks again. It's made out of an old oil drum, and with a fire roaring inside, the barrel literally turns "red hot" and so do the pipes stringing across the kitchen ceiling.

She makes herself a peanut butter sandwich and watches

TV, but eventually shuts off the television in order to hear the car motor. For a while, she loses herself in the stories in her reader. Around 10:00, making sure that the fire has become embers, she goes to bed in her clothes and soon sleeps.

She's in a nightmare, with the three little pigs and the wolf hammering on the door. When she opens her eyes she realizes that the pounding is real. Mr. Morten bursts into the room. "Lazy girl!" he snarls. "Shleeping. Should be cooking."

Melda shrinks into the corner, pulling the quilt to her chin.

"I'll forgive you," he says, "if you show me a little affection." He falls on his knees, his arms reaching for her across the bed.

Every square inch of Melda's skin cringes away from him. His breath is asphyxiating. He flops onto the bed like a fish, then lies quiet, overcome with exertion and alcohol. He coughs. Maybe he's going to vomit. Melda glances at the porch door leading outside. It's bolted. The bolt wouldn't budge when she tried it a few days earlier. Can she force it? She's thankful she's dressed – though her shoes are on the far side of the bed.

She springs up, seizes the bolt, forces it back, and shoves the outer door open.

"Hey? Where you goin'?" Mr. Morten rears up, but she is gone, falling two feet down onto the wet grass, so icy on her socks. She runs around the house to get her duck boots on the veranda. Where can she go? The car? No. If he pursues her, he'll look there. She grabs the blanket on the back seat and wraps it around herself.

She can see the mailbox and not much else. Then the clouds shift and the moon appears, full and round. It sails ahead of her, pulling her down the road. Then she thinks of the school. Only three miles away. She will hide outside until the janitor opens the doors. Then, at recess, she will tell Mrs. Abbott about Mr. Morten, and get them to phone her social worker. "Goodbye Aspen Grove School," she thinks. "I can't go on like this."

When she reaches the school she is whimpering. The moon is under a cloud but the yard light illuminates the building, so stern and square, with two tiny windows under the side slopes of the roof. One is in the tiny principal's office on the east side, halfway up the stairs to the second story. On the opposite side is an identical room for the public health nurse's infrequent visits.

Wrapped in her blanket, she huddles on the rear fire escape, watching the dawn. When the custodian arrives, he opens the girls' door first, and she creeps in and tiptoes downstairs to the girls' washroom. An abandoned comb on the towel dispenser will do for her hair; then she uses hand soap and paper towels to clean herself up. She tucks in her shirt, shakes out her sweater, wipes the mud from her boots, and folds the blanket and leaves it on the bench outside the door.

She thinks of the apple on Mrs. Abbott's desk, and tiptoes to try the classroom door. Usually Mr. Flynn and Mrs. Abbott lock and unlock their own classrooms, but today Mrs. Abbott's is open.

Melda eats the apple in the girls' entry-way. When the first bus arrives, she slips away to the washroom, until the children have spread out through the school. Then she goes to the hallway outside the two classrooms and looks out the big windows. Where is Mrs. Abbott? She's usually here before the first bus arrives. As Melda watches, an old Nash Rambler rolls into the school lane and from it emerge two large gray-haired women.

Cheryl, who has joined her, lets out a moan. "Oh, God, the Stickney sisters! There's a teachers' meeting and they've come to fill in." These teachers are now retired, and Cheryl hates when they're called in because all they care about is keeping order. She likes substitutes who have art all day.

Melda could weep. Mr. Flynn and Mrs. Abbott are away! Her plan to report the Mortens must wait. Could she ask to use the phone in Mr. Flynn's office? No. The elder Miss Stickney will demand to know the reason. Besides, she will never get through to Miss Fowler; a secretary will want the number to call her back. It's hopeless!

The Mortens won't miss her immediately. They'll still be sleeping it off, and when they get up, will assume that she has gone to school. If she doesn't show up tonight, they'll think she's at Cheryl's place and that they've forgotten.

During Math, Melda realizes that her books are at the

Mortens. Luckily she has good eyesight and Miss Stickney doesn't. Melda reads the math questions over Cheryl's shoulder, and sings out the correct answers as required. She borrows a reader. At lunch, she tells Cheryl that she has forgotten her sandwiches, and Cheryl shares hers. In the afternoon she can snooze while Miss Stickney listens to the other grades read.

When the day is almost over, the supply teacher, armed with a pointer, walks down the aisle in her orthopedic Oxfords. She stops at Melda's desk.

"You're the 'Home girl' who lives at the Mortens," she booms, peering at her through bifocals. Melda wishes for a burrow to crawl into. She nods.

"How do you like it there?"

"Fine," Melda whispers automatically.

At 3:30 she hides in the washroom again, as the buses leave. Should she have told Miss Stickney the truth about the Mortens? Has she wasted an opportunity? The patter of feet has subsided; the last bus has rolled away, and now is her chance. If the principal's office is unlocked, she will try to reach her social worker. She tiptoes up the stairs, reaching the office landing. Huddling at the newel post she hears Miss Stickney speaking. *She's on the phone.*

"Ethel? Sister?" The other Miss Stickney is in the main hallway calling up the stairs. Melda crawls up the six steps to the hall outside the auditorium, then scoots past the doors and down the six steps on the other side to the nurse's room. Locked! She crouches on the turn. Finally, the elder Miss Stickney clipclops down to the main floor, and together they leave the school.

Melda pads softly downstairs and eases into Mrs. Abbott's room. The janitor has swept it, and won't be back. She locks the Yale, noting how to keep it unlocked when she goes out to the washroom later.

In one desk she finds a peanut butter sandwich, an apple and some Halloween kisses. She crouches behind the sand table to eat, holding her breath as the custodian leaves the school. As his tires crunch on the gravel, Melda feels almost happy. At Mrs. Abbott's desk she looks at the daughters' faces. She opens a reader and presents "Silver" to an imaginary class.

If she were a teacher — what a hope! — she would be like Mrs. Abbott. To become a teacher you had to get good grades, and Melda finds that harder and harder. Now, exhausted, she takes the reader to the cloakroom, where she puts on the star-spangled bed jacket and lies on a pile of costumes. Soon she is asleep.

She wakes and sees the clock-face in a shaft of moonlight. The washroom? Way down those dark stairs? Yes! Carefully adjusting the lock, she leaves the classroom, her footsteps echoing. Through the hall windows she notices a glow in the sky. Northern Lights? She rushes downstairs, shivering.

Back upstairs, she draws the bed jacket around her and falls asleep on the teddy bear costumes. She dreams of Grandma, bending over her for a good night kiss. "Don't go!" she cries, and holds out her arms. But it is not a dream. The face above hers is... Grandma's? No, Mrs. Abbott's.

"She's here!" Mrs. Abbott gathers Melda into her arms. Mr. Abbott and Mr. Flynn join them.

"What's up?" asks Melda. No one speaks. Then Mrs. Abbott says that they have been looking all over for her. There has been a fire at the Mortens. The Abbotts and Mr. Flynn were returning from town along the boundary road when they saw the light in the sky. Then they found the house ablaze, with neighbours standing helplessly by.

"What about the Mortens?" Melda asks. Mrs. Abbott hesitates, then says that they have been taken to hospital. "We didn't know where you were," she adds. "Cheryl said you didn't come home on the bus tonight, so we hoped..."

Melda plasters herself against Mrs. Abbott. "I don't want to leave this school."

"Of course not," said Mrs. Abbott. "We'll work something out. Now, you're coming home with us. Who has a coat?" As Mr. Flynn takes off his windbreaker, Melda pins her arms to her body. She can't leave the bed jacket behind.

Mrs. Abbott puts the windbreaker around Melda's shoulders and takes her hand as she leads her to the truck.

and now the trees

James McLaughlin

look less like the lines we drew
as children
with our smiling, uneasy hands

there were complex root structures in the dirt we
    never saw

now the sky's full of more lines than we ever drew as
children under the trees,
and we're both taller now
with too many lines to draw every year:
the trees
grow up faster than we can be children.

The Boy Who Loved to Fish

Bruce Lader

He didn't fathom a word of English,
wanted his South Korean home.
I *dunno*, *I dunno*, he hid in fear

so his tutor gave him a map of Earth,
a recorder to breathe anywhere free,
become boss of whistles, Simon Says.

They explored crocodile rivers,
barracuda and marlin thrashed the seas,
trout sailed; the world grew less ominous

until another boy pushed him overboard
in school, and anger swallowed
the new words in his mouth. Life got sad.

With a calculator faster than the tutor,
he found laughter on an island
of numbers. Surprised he was back

the fish greeted him with singing,
chanted rhythms of English together,
introduced him to heroes from the planet

he needed to study, asked him to draw
muscular letters so they could play baseball
and golf, bike ride with feet on handlebars.

When the boy watered the tree he planted,
sentences sprouted like minnows in April,
he knew how to talk with every fish.

Out of Line

Mad Kids

Mary Barrett

we went straight to the horse chestnuts
shucked from their sharp spiked shells,

burnished brown, hard as river rock,

hurled to hurt

across the great expanse of ground
raked clean of fall turning leaves;

one knocked part of my brother's front tooth out,
the jagged tooth a demarcation line

from that time until now
an end to horse chestnut war.

Praying at Cook Road Mosque

Elizabeth Ann James

It glitters. Snow as fine as baking powder
flies against the glass door of the alcove
where we leave our shoes. Suede boots gelly straps
gold sandals & fitness clogs form a line
outside the big room where the women pray.
The oatmeal rug seems warm under us
strangely resembles a stretch of sand
at dawn.   Swathed in warm dark colors wools silks
paisleys the women remind me of The Pillars
when they stand I imagine they cast shadows
when they bow down they form humps
Asia comes in late
pulling on her white cotton skirt
so that her jeans don't show see how she's snapping
the white muslin head veil under her chin
—Leeza Miriam Nabihya Wiffan
Callie Namsatch —On a necklace of praying women
here I am
praying where I sit in a folding chair behind everyone
my palms open on my knees I try to stare
at a spot on the rug pay attention to my breaths I
imagine I can hear all of us breathing all
of us breathing. Outdoors I'd blow steam
imagine pale red ice clouds drifting from
mass graves in Mexico Kosovo Belgrade I'd see
childhood gardens in Haifa
The Mountain jasmine flowers candlelight
The Koran pours gold coins melting
from the loudspeaker in the small room where the men
     pray.
Soon the new hall will be ready and " the ladies" will sit
in a new space behind the men. "Modesty

143

& required mode of supplication" require this yet
I will remember tonight fifth of Ramadan.
We women our dark clothes the discs of bread
sand & snow glittering behind my closed eyes
while I sit with other women at the edge
of the big room where none but women pray.
I like it this way best.

Two Women

Anne Da Vigo

Naomi called at 10. "I'm awake now. I want my oatmeal and honey. I want coffee."

Mary Guyton held her cell phone with one strong, brown hand and slipped a bookmark into the Bible. "You be a rude, arrogant woman, sure," she said. Mary heard a crackle in her ear, which meant the old lady was exhaling cigarette smoke.

"I don't need to be polite. You're my employee," Naomi said.

If Mary were still on St. Vincent, she'd get even by asking her old *tante* to whack the head off a chicken and scatter the blood. Hexes really worked in the Caribbean, but she was doubtful about New Jersey.

"I'll be there. Half an hour." She gave the "End" button a stab with her thumb and studied the telephone as if the small screen might display a bit of otherworldly advice.

After a minute, she speed-dialed Jim Montigue. "I'm quitting at the end of the week. Senior Care can find another nurse." She got her chops in before Jim had a chance to identify himself.

"Now Mary, it's not that easy to find people." Jim was lazy, a semi-retired Virginia boy who didn't want the bother of hunting down a new nurse for his difficult client. "I need you. Naomi needs you. The last nurse sweet-talked Naomi out of three paintings worth about half a million. And he came with such good recommendations."

"Your problems are not my problems. Get to work on it." Mary put her phone in her purse. By long-familiar touch, she rolled her hair into a fat sausage at the back of her head. Once a month, she visited the Clairol bottle. She wanted her hair black like an onyx ring, darker than her brown-black skin. Her husband, Andre, had lots of white hairs, but he refused to put dye on them.

The tires of her station-wagon car crunched on the ice and road salt as she drove between Trenton and Princeton. She passed

145

the red-brick hospital where she worked two days a week with geriatric patients. The edges of the building's roof dripped with icicles.

On the car radio, all the stations had bad news about President George W. wanting to go to war with Iraq. She sighed, shook her shoulders to banish her gloomy feelings and pushed the heater control to "High." She missed the Caribbean the most at this time of year. February in St. Vincent landed as light as a bird feather, all sun and breeze and tender leaves.

Mary parked in Naomi's driveway. The walk hadn't been shoveled and yesterday's snow had turned icy. She'd get Andre over here tonight to shovel after he finished work. Her key clicked in the deadbolt. Other than Naomi's lawyer, only Mary and the other nurse kept keys.

She closed the door and was imprisoned again by the strange atmosphere of the house, the air thick with the smell of nicotine and the walls crowded with paintings, the tabletops with sculptures. Fastened to the wall above the fireplace like a stag's head was a white sculpture of a nude woman's torso. Mary avoided looking at it, not so much because of the missing head and limbs, but because it seemed shameful to display the mutilated woman's genitals and small breasts.

The portable TV yammered in the kitchen, but when Mary peered in she saw it was jinxed again. The weatherman's face shone the color of green bananas. "There's a storm warning out in the Delaware Valley, and we might get four to five inches by mid-afternoon."

Sound drifted down from upstairs, where the big TV in Naomi's bedroom had the same channel on. "Naomi. I'm here," Mary called. She hung up her coat and climbed the carpeted steps, past the disturbing drawings of women with open mouths. Naomi told her they were valuable etchings by Picasso.

In the bedroom, Naomi sat in her wheelchair, smoking and stroking Topaz. The cat jumped down from Naomi's bony lap and rubbed his gray side against Mary's ankle. Cat hair plastered itself to the hem of her navy blue slacks.

146

The bedroom walls were stained yellow-brown with cigarette smoke. No paintings hung on these walls, only photographs of Bill, some of them from when he was young, looking like a starving artist, with a lock of wavy hair falling over his forehead. A drawing done by somebody famous showed a mature Bill wearing glasses.

On the marble-topped dresser perched a picture of Naomi's sister sitting on a garden bench in the yard of a two-story house. "Jewish-American princesses from Brooklyn, that's us," Naomi had said.

Naomi looked thinner today, her cheeks sinking like a dip in the snow. Her white hair swept back from her forehead in a transparent veil, showing pink scalp underneath. Old she was, 93 or 94, but she didn't have a wrinkle in her infuriating face. Her sea-blue eyes shone clear and her nose was thin, not thickened on the tip like some old people.

"You took your time. My boyfriend is hungry." Naomi tilted her chin and formed her lips in a puckery "o" to blow the smoke out. Mary had quit smoking after she met Andre, a Seventh-Day Adventist, but sometimes she longed to feel a cigarette between her lips.

"What, you can't walk downstairs and get him some food? I left an open can of Fancy Feast in the refrigerator yesterday. " Mary smoothed the rumpled sheets on Naomi's twin bed and shook the feather pillow. The other bed was made up, as though Bill were about to pull back the bedspread and climb under the blankets. He'd been dead for 25 years.

"I'll do no such thing. You are here to do my bidding," Naomi said.

"Oh, am I? Your servant? And you are the queen of what country?" Mary slid her hand under Topaz' stomach, tucked him under her arm and carried him, yowling, down to the kitchen. Topaz jumped out of her arms and scolded her while she washed her hands in the sink. She filled a pan with water for the oatmeal and put it on the stove. Only one of the burners worked.

"Okay, lover. Your turn." She scraped the remains of the cat food from the can to a china saucer.

"What kind is that?" Naomi called.

"Chicken."

"Don't give him that. Give him salmon."

"You're very bossy today, sure," Mary called up the stair-well. She returned to the kitchen and put the saucer of chicken on the floor. "I had a cat once, when I lived in Brooklyn." Topaz looked up, his fangs showing as he chewed. "It was a pretty little thing, black and white. Andre never liked it. I loaned it to my sister to catch some rats. Then she loaned it to a friend and it disappeared."

Mary tore open a packet of Earl Grey. "I was vex at my sister. She gave it away without asking. I say to her, I say, 'She ate it. That old woman cooked my cat for supper.'"

"Don't forget the honey," Naomi said. Her voice echoed now as she maneuvered to the stair landing. Her three-footed aluminum cane clanked. Mary climbed the stairs, stood on Naomi's strong side and guided her down, an arm around her body. Naomi's ribs were held together by no more flesh than a skinny chicken. At the kitchen table, the old lady sank into a chair, breathing heavily.

"Is Yoko coming today?" Mary spooned the thick oatmeal into a dish, drizzled honey over the top and set the dish, a folded paper napkin and a stainless steel spoon on the Formica tabletop.

"Not today. She's in London for a show."

"This Yoko Uno—she John Lennon's wife, yes?" Mary poured her tea. She sometimes tried to categorize the various artists Naomi had known like index cards in her mind; but just when she thought she had them all arranged, she forgot the names again.

"A friend of Bill's," Naomi said, "from our New York days. Once upon a time we did art but not any more. My color vision is fading. Now we're just two old ladies who talk about how things used to be." Naomi rolled a bite in her mouth and her throat worked to swallow. Mary reached across the table and whisked away an oatmeal speck from her chin with a paper napkin.

"Bill, how long were you married to him?"

A bloom crept up Naomi's cheekbones, and the old lady faded, like a scene on TV dissolving, and Mary saw the woman that

Naomi had been when she was young, her hair red like Scarlett O'Hara.

"Thirty-two years. Well, we weren't married all that time. Not when we lived in the Village." Her upper lip swelled, full and pink, as if she were thinking about sex. Did women that old still remember what sex was like?

"Ah. You thought he was good looking?"

"Oh, yes. The women were always falling in love with him, especially his students. It was his wavy hair." Naomi's long fingers dipped over her own forehead. "I invited them to dinner so I could keep my eye on them."

Mary thought about the pictures of Bill in the bedroom. He had a white man's face with a long nose and thin lips. His nose and sharp chin didn't quite line up, like shirt buttons offset from the belt buckle.

Mary imagined them as artists in the 1930s, drinking bitter red wine in a Greenwich Village party, cigarette smoke swirling, saxophone playing on the radio. Men wearing blue denim shirts and wide neckties printed with hibiscus. She wondered how Naomi had met Bill.

Mary had met Andre in Brooklyn in the 1980s, and he was as different from her first husband, Henri, as New York was from St. Vincent. Henri had been a big man, but light skinned, the color of caramel. They operated a restaurant in St. Vincent on a white sand beach near the harbor. Visitors who sailed there on their yachts bought Mary's spicy pork, black beans and rice, and fried bananas soaked in rum. He had an eye for the women, Henri did. When that deep, dangerous note crept into his voice as he waited on a woman at the counter, her chest contracted in pain. The day finally came when she left him, shook his dust off her shoes. Like Jesus told the disciples when people rejected them. She'd taken a plane to Brooklyn and moved in with her sister, Celeste.

Mary first laid eyes on Andre in the video store where she worked, filling in for Celeste while she went to Saturday services at the Seventh Day Adventist Church. Mary knew she wanted him. His skin gleamed as dark as a moonless night on the islands. Her mother would have folded her arms and turned her back on him, but here on the mainland, dark and light didn't matter so much.

"Why are you working on the Sabbath?" he said.

"For the money. The landlord, he is so inconsiderate as to charge me rent," she said, and reached around him to take two dollars from a customer.

"Have you read *Steps to Christ* by Ellen G. White?" Andre asked her, leaning against the counter. Light reflected off his full lips, and she thought about sweat and rumpled sheets.

"What do you think? Here I am, taking people's money on the Seventh Day." Mary had a quick mouth, but she liked that righteousness that Andre wore like a pair of old shoes.

He looked at her, as if trying to find all her hidden parts and put them together in a jigsaw puzzle. "I'll loan it to you," he said, but he didn't call the first week, not for three weeks. He'd had to order the book, he told her later.

Naomi tapped her spoon against the side of the bowl. "How about earning your pay?"

"What? Oh, yes." Mary selected four tablets from the "Tuesday" compartment of Naomi's pill organizer and lined them up beside her water glass.

"Get my address book from the study. I need the telephone number of Bill's editor." She was editing some of his papers into another book.

Late in the afternoon, Jim called. "I think I might have found someone. You remember Rita Longworth? She's available."

"You mocking me?"

"No, really." Jim's voice was bland.

"The hospital refuses to hire her back. She made too many mistakes with the medications when she was drinking." Rita had given the old man on Three West too much Respordal and he never sat up again.

"She's turned herself around. She's going to AA."

"I suppose they take attendance there," Mary said.

"Rita says she can start with Saturday's shift."

"You're not fooling me, you know. I see what you're doing."

She stayed, of course.

# # #

Eight months later, the first thing Mary saw when her eyes opened was the abstract white and black painting on Naomi's recreation room wall. Of the dozens in Naomi's collection, it was the only one Mary liked.

The metal hide-a-bed frame creaked as she propped herself on one elbow. She saw all kinds of stories in the painting, like she did when she looked at clouds as a child. It was large, four by seven feet. In the upper right you could see a hospital patient if you held your head at the correct angle. The patient was a small black man wrapped in a white sheet. He was propped with his back against the headboard. And up there on the left, the nurse sat at her desk. She wore a white cap, like nurses did forty years ago.

Mary swung out of bed, the floor cold beneath the soles of her feet. She worked twenty-four-hour duty four days a week now, while the other nurse did three days. It took an hour in the morning to ease her sore back from the bad mattress. When she climbed the stairs, she saw Naomi still sleeping, her mouth open, breath like a rough wave as it passed her lips. The TV showed a travelogue about a Pacific island. It had a volcano like La Soufriere on St. Vincent, but not as dramatic.

In the kitchen, Mary made her cup of Earl Grey. She held the warm mug in her palms and propped her elbows on the counter beside the sink. Leaves on the birch trees outside the window shone like gold teeth in the autumn sun. Naomi never came downstairs now. Mary carried her meals up and served her on a tray table beside a rented hospital bed.

The doorbell rang. Through the peephole, Mary saw the crown of a woman's head. Millicent. A far-away cousin of Bill's and co-conservator for Naomi's personal care.

Mary turned the deadbolt and opened the door. She didn't have to ask permission from the lawyers to let Millicent in.

"Mary. You're looking…prosperous." Millicent had a long nose, a round, melon stomach and gray hair. She reminded Mary of the possum that lived in the vacant lot near her house. Some nights in the alley the plump creature would hiss and show its yellow fangs at her when she emptied the garbage.

Millicent surveyed the living room, checking the paintings and sculpture. Mary suspected Millicent was taking inventory to make sure the black nurse hadn't stolen anything.

"I'm not sure if Naomi's awake yet. Let me check."

Naomi turned her head as Mary approached the bed. "I heard someone come in. It's Katherine's girl?" Naomi signaled Mary to raise the head of the bed.

"You need to use the toilet?"

"Not now. I want my glasses. Be quick about it." Mary fitted the temple pieces over Naomi's ears and brushed her hair, careful not to scratch her scalp with the bristles.

Naomi looked at Millicent critically as the younger woman perched on the edge of the wing chair, her hands clasped in her lap. "What, your mother won't give you a dress from her shop? You have to buy at the thrift store?" Naomi was her old self, eyes gleaming with malice. The first time in over a week. Millicent blinked rapidly. "You're not walking now? You're in bed all the time?"

"I stay in bed when I feel like it. To rest my derriere. I'm perfectly capable of getting up." Naomi slid Mary a sly look out of the side of her glasses. "Where are my cigarettes?"

Millicent stared in horror. "You're still smoking? In your condition?"

"Cigarettes. And a can of Ensure." A wicked twitch hovered at the corner of Naomi's mouth.

"Okay," Mary said.

Millicent's eyes rolled up, as if shocked at Mary's permissiveness. "I should never have moved to Poughkepsie," she said to Naomi. "Without a car, I can't visit often enough to monitor your care, Naomi."

Mary scraped the sharp edge of the tab against the metal Ensure can. *Try caring for a rich, sick, mean old woman yourself sometime.* She wasn't gong to fight with a failing patient over a few cigarettes.

"So, how is Katherine?" Smoke drifted out Naomi's nose.

"Mamma had to give up the shop. Too many debts."

"Too much scotch, I'd say." Naomi chuckled. "Is all of your grandfather's money gone?"

Millicent's chest rose with a deep breath. "Actually, I bring wonderful news. Mamma has accepted Jesus Christ."

"Isn't that nice," Naomi said, momentarily distracted by a volcano eruption on TV.

"I'd like to bring Pastor Milliken by to talk to you. About accepting Christ as your personal savior," Millicent said.

Naomi's eyes grew huge. "I'm a Jew who doesn't go to synagogue. I don't want to see any Pastor Milliken."

"You're nearing the end of your time. Don't you want eternal life?"

"Up there in the clouds? With the angels playing harps? I don't know. I've never looked good in white," Naomi said.

Mary sat on the other twin bed, her folded arms resting on her knees, to watch the verbal sparring. *That's it, you old crone. Give her what-for*.

Millicent scanned the display of photographs. "You want to see Bill again, don't you?"

"Bill?"

"Yes. He has been raised from the dead and sits with Jesus Christ in heaven."

Naomi's hand trembled. "He's not alive. He died of leukemia. He weighed one hundred and seventeen pounds and I didn't recognize him in his coffin."

Mary leaned over to take the Ensure can from Naomi and set it on the tray table.

"The two of you could be rejoined in eternal bliss if you are baptized in the Christian faith and repent of your sins," Millicent said. "Think what it would be like, to be with him forever."

Smoke from Naomi's cigarette drifted into her eyes. "I don't know. I've never believed in God."

"Bill would be waiting for you. To welcome you to heaven," Millicent said. The tip of her nose twitched eagerly, as if she'd caught the scent of her next meal.

Mary looked down at her lap. Her hands had curled into fists in her pink palms. Should she intervene? Mary was all for people coming to Jesus, praise the Lord, but somehow she didn't think the Lord would like this scene.

Naomi's legs moved restlessly under the blanket. "Are you all right?" Mary asked. "Is your tail bone sore?" Mary slid a pillow into the small of Naomi's back.

"Uh-oh," Naomi said. Mary frowned, then touched the sheet under Naomi's thighs. It was wet with warm urine.

"What happened? I thought you didn't have to go," Mary said.

Naomi's brows drew together as if searching for the answer. "A man came in and threw a bucket of water on me?"

Mary took the cigarette from Naomi's fingers and stubbed it out in the ashtray. "Excuse us. We need to clean up." She put her hand on the bedroom doorknob, waiting for Millicent to leave.

"I'll be back this evening. Meanwhile, I'm going to ask Jim for an inventory of the paintings and sculpture," Millicent said.

####

It was winter again, and Mary slept in Bill's bed. Topaz woke her on his morning stroll across her face. His hungry mewlings provided a backbeat to the irritating hum of the oxygen machine. Out the window, light streaked the sky with pale yellow.

Mary stared at the walls for a minute, counting the pictures of Bill. Fourteen. In her sleepy state, Bill seemed like God, surveying the world with a crooked grin. Mary twisted her head and peered at the other bed.

Naomi's eyes were open but unseeing, looking beyond this world toward the mysterious universe. Air tubes crawled up her nose. Breath drifted slowly past her lips. It was as though her lungs inflated thoughtfully, considering if they should gather themselves for another respiration.

Mary crossed to Naomi's bed, lowered the aluminum railing and slid her fingers over Naomi's pulse point. Thready. The old woman was close. Another hour or two perhaps.

Mary stroked her thumb softly over Naomi's bottom lip. It had cracked from the dryness. A thin line of congealed blood marked the course of the broken skin. Mary slipped on her green felt slippers and padded down to the kitchen. She popped open the refrigerator's freezer and plucked out two little Popsicles of frozen water on a white stick.

When she returned, Naomi hadn't moved. "Here, girlfriend. This make you more comfortable." She painted Naomi's lips with the ice and watched as droplets formed from the faint heat of the old woman's skin. When her lips were wet, Mary slipped the cool treat between Naomi's teeth and ran it over her tongue and the lining of her mouth.

"Doesn't that feel good?" she crooned, as if Naomi were the baby Mary had never had. Naomi's eyelids slid shut for a second like an acknowledgment. Mary checked the diaper between Naomi's legs. It was barely wet. Her kidneys were shutting down. Mary flexed her knees and slipped her forearms under Naomi to shift her onto her side. The familiar odors of age clung to her: brittle hair, flakes of skin, threads of her old nightgown. Mary made notations on Naomi's chart and left a message with the physician's answering machine concerning her condition.

In the kitchen, Topaz leaped to the shelf in a puff of cat hair. She opened a fresh tin of salmon. "Even the wicked can get lonely, is that it?"

She pursed her full lips and blew on her tea. Her fingers leafed through the Bible's onionskin pages until she found the Twenty-third Psalm.

Her cell phone interrupted her reading. "Mary, it's Jim. Millicent has arrived in town. We're goin' to stop by and pick up the most valuable paintings for safekeeping."

She was surprised to look down and see the delicate page crumpled in her fingers. "You did an inventory last year on everything valuable. What, you think I'm going to hide a work of art in my overnight bag?"

Jim cleared his throat. "Millicent is concerned about theft. Who knows? Someone might break in."

"Taking the pictures away would be bad for Naomi," Mary said. "She's not dead yet, and other than the memory of her husband, they're all she's got." Mary remembered a story she had once read about a dying man's relatives fighting over his furniture. "She'll be gone by tomorrow. Wait a day."

"Don't be so sensitive. Naomi's comatose. She'll never realize they're gone."

"She'll know. The house will be filled with indignity," Mary said.

But Millicent and Jim came anyway. They stripped the pieces off the walls, leaving pale rectangles like the bald white heads of chemotherapy patients. Millicent's eyes glistened. Naomi must have changed her will and left Millicent something.

After the paintings were stowed in Jim's van, the three of them gathered beside Naomi's bed. "I'm surprised you're leaving her false teeth in," he said.

About six, Andre arrived with two containers of garlic chicken and rice. The squeak of the Styrofoam boxes startled Mary as Andre pried open the lids. For hours, the only sound Mary had heard was the oxygen machine. "The old lady, she is still with us?" Andre asked.

"She's holding on. She is a stubborn, stubborn woman," Mary said.

Andre studied her with a humorous quiver of his lips.

"No, I'm not. Stubborn, no," Mary said. More and more often now, she and Andre communicated wordlessly.

After dinner, she washed the forks and wiped off the table. "I'm going up to check on her. Why don't you come?" The stairs creaked under their weight as they passed the spots where the Picassos had hung. Mary and Andre looked at her, their shoulders touching. Naomi's skin had a blue undertone, like snow under the trees. Almost a minute passed, the only sound the labored breath of the oxygen machine.

Finally, Naomi's chest rose under her flannel nightgown. The neckline was rumpled and Mary straightened it, letting her fingers rest on Naomi's collarbone. Strangely, it didn't surprise Mary when Naomi turned her head a fraction. "Bill's here?" she whispered.

"No, honey, it's Andre. He's come to say hello."

"Oh, yes. Andre." Her tongue moved in her dry mouth. "Mary?"

"Yes."

"He's very like Bill." Her head sank into the pillow, and this time, no breath.

Out of Line

IV

LIVING IN DIFFERENT WORLDS

Olive in Two Languages

Louise Domaratius

Olive likes saying her name in English: *AH-Liv*. It's in Henry James, Maman said, and his Olive is a very pretty lady. In French it's nothing but a little, shiny, round fruit: *O-LEEV.* Accent on the second syllable, please. She prefers herself in English: the beautiful lady, *la belle dame.* Besides, when you switch the letters around, they make *I Love.*

"Olive" is also for the Mediterranean, Mamam said. For the sea and peace and Greek temples all sparkling in the sun. Daddy's the one who chose her name, before she was born even.

She clings to the memory now of what it was like, when he held her in his arms. She would ride around on his shoulders and smell the clean, white laundry smell of his office shirt. *Son bleu de travail,* he used to joke. His work overalls. Daddy's French was good, but he was English. That's why Olive speaks English.

"*Je parle anglais. Et vous? Do you speak English, Monsieur?*"

"A little," the man said. It sounded like "a LEEtle," like the end of her name, the French way. He was sitting on a bench in the park, and beside him was a huge canvas backpack, all out of shape and torn and discolored. He had his arm around it, like a fiancée.

"What's in your bag, Monsieur?" Olive asked.

"Leetle girl curiosity, eh?" asked the man. His complexion was brown and his cheeks a little hollow. Spiky black bristles stood out on his chin and above his upper lip. He smiled at Olive, and the white of his teeth flashed just like one of those sunlit Greek columns. It made her feel warm. Mediterranean sun.

Calais was chilly in November. Maman had made her wear

her dove-gray anorak, the one with the fake-fur collar and the pink lining. "Remember, I can see you from the balcony," she'd said to Olive. "You can walk along the pyracantha, but don't go away from the fence. *C'est promis?*"

"I promise." Olive had said. Pyracantha; that meant firethorn. She'd gathered up a whole hankyful of bright, orange-red berries from the bushes near the black fence, the wrought-iron grille. If she could find a squirrel, she would try and feed them to it. That was when she'd seen the man. He looked tired and discouraged and very poor.

"In my bag," he said, answering Olive's question, "are everything I need for England."

"Vous allez en Angleterre?" Olive was so surprised, she lapsed back into French. He didn't look like the tourists that climbed on the ferry. "Is that your suitcase? And your guidebook? Do you have one?"

The man smiled again, his warm sun smile, and said no, he didn't have any need of a guidebook. He knew someone who was going to show him the way. He was going to England to stay, forever. And then to bring his family. His wife, his little girl. A little girl like Olive, but with black hair, not golden.

"Why aren't they with you now?" Olive asked, suddenly distressed. Another daddy, going to England. Maybe like hers, he would never call for his little girl.

"Treep too deeficult," he said. "Later, they come. When I get work and money, lots of money to pay for passage."

"Please, what's her name? *Elle s'appelle comment, votre fille?*"

" Sorayya her name," he said. "You want see peecture? I show you, Meess." From the depths of his battered bag, he drew a small plastic square. It was a little greasy-blurry, like Maman's glasses, when she'd accidentally put a finger on the lenses. Through the smudgy plastic, a little girl stared. She had very big, very serious black eyes. A navy blue scarf covered most of her hair, and two ends of it crossed beneath her chin.

"Why does she have a scarf? Is it cold where you're from?"

"Tradeetion. Sometimes cold, sometimes not. In England,

she no wear scarf. Be like English girls. Wind in hair. Hair fly like blackbird weeng. Here bracelet from her. I keep to think of her." From an outer pocket of the backpack, he pulled a tarnished, copper-colored circlet.

"Don't you miss her?"

"Very much, I meess."

"Why didn't you stay with her?" In spite of herself, Olive felt something tight in her throat when she asked this.

"No good for leetle girls in my country. Bad men break everytheeng. In England, everytheeng good. Lots work for poor men. Nice people, don' ask for papers all day long. Cheeldren go to school. Good food to eat."

" *Olive! Dépeche-toi! Hurry up!*" Mamam was calling.

Olive heard her name, s*on nom français.* She had to go back. "Is your boat tonight?" she asked the man.

"I don' theenk so."

" Then where will you go? Will you get your supper?"

The man shook his head. "I sleep here. Nice park, nice bench. But cold in France. Sangatte center shut, they don' let me een. So I wait here. Wait for friend who show me the way."

"O-LEEV!"

"Au revoir, Monsieur. Bye-bye!"

Olive looked both ways and ran to the apartment building across the street.

****

She had a crusty *baguette* for the backpack man, the kind she liked best, with the inside all soft-white and chewy. She'd saved her chocolate from her four o'clock *goûter,* and Maman would never notice the missing apples. Olive had had an idea last night, before she'd fallen asleep. Let him still be here, she'd thought, as she drifted off. Please let him still be here. Let him not be gone, not yet, *pas encore, pas encore…*

He was there, the deep tan of his face slightly ruddy in the cold afternoon light, the black bristles of his chin a little longer. He smiled his marble-white sun smile at Olive and took the bread with a "Thank you, leetle mademoiselle."

"Monsieur, Sir, please, pretty please, *s'il vous plaît,*" she said, "will you do something for me?"

"What can I do for you?" he asked, his black eyebrows puzzling together.

"When you are in England…"

"Yes…?"

"When you are in England, will you look for my daddy for me and give him a message?"

"Your daddy in Eengland?"

"Yes."

"Eengland very beeg place. Where I look? London?"

"Yes, London. Mr. Donald Davenport. And my name is Olive." She said AH-liv. "Tell him I want him to have me come. Like Sorayya, for you. Please, will you?"

"I don' understand. Your daddy in Eengland; he don' call for you? You don' veezit?"

Olive's eyes filled, and the man stopped his questions.

"You don' cry," he said, touching her hand. "I look for daddy for you. Write name on piece paper, OK?"

****

On Wednesday, there was no school in the afternoon, and Olive went earlier to the park, but on the bench were two teenagers from the *lycée,* the high school down the street. As the girl leaned toward the boy to offer her mouth for kissing, her tight, short pullover rode up and showed the pale skin of her back. The boy had sticky-pointy hair and a wide leather belt. A backpack sat beside him, but it wasn't like the man's. Olive moved toward it, though, her heart beating, as if staring at this new khaki bag would transform it into the man's old, gray one.

The boy looked at her over his girlfriend's shoulder. "Hey, little girl, what do you want?" he asked.

"Have you … has either of you seen a man around here? A dark-haired monsieur with a beat-up backpack?"

"What do you want with this man and his backpack?"

" Nothing…" Olive didn't know what to say. They were

squatting in his place. Maybe he wasn't far, but she wasn't supposed to go beyond the firethorn. Then she spotted it: a newspaper-wrapped lump under the bench.

" Excuse me," she said to the two high school kids, kneeling down abruptly in front of the bench and stretching out her arm to grab the package. Her name was scrawled on it, spelled right, the way she'd written it for the man: OLIVE DAVENPORT. She snatched the newspaper and held it to her chest.

"It was someone… a foreign monsieur… he wanted to go to England." She was still on her knees beside the boy and girl, clutching the small packet.

They were both looking at her now.

"*Un clandestin?*" the girl asked. An illegal?

"What's an illegal?"

"A refugee, one who sneaked in," the girl told her. "The police cleaned up last night. They put them all on a coach for I don't know where. Some of them are going to ask for asylum in France. Others are going back to where they came from."

"Back home?" Olive's voice caught.

"So what? What is it to you?"

"Then, they won't be going to England?" Olive asked. Already she could feel the rush of tears behind her eyes, pressing against them like a curtain of oncoming rain.

The girl shrugged and looked at the boy. "Probably not. England doesn't want them." They watched her take off like an arrow, dash past the ardent hedge of prickly bush.

****

In the refuge of her bedroom, Olive unfolded the sheets of newspaper with care. Over and over she rubbed Soraya's slender bracelet between her palms, pressing her nose to the warm metal smell. Then she put it away, ever so carefully, between two leaves of the album where she kept the photographs of Daddy and AH-liv, bouncing on his knee, riding on his shoulders.

Sparrows Falling from the Sky

Christine Swanberg

The soprano, whose voice is brilliant
As fire, sings the aria from Madam Butterfly
On the radio in the Port Townsend Antique Store.

The notes build like snow before an avalanche
On Mount Baker across the bay.
This could be heaven, I am thinking

Examining the quirky Nippon vases
I have grown fond of: the ardor of their attempts
At European Baroque foiled

By the ever- graceful elongated necks
Of snow geese, the calligraphy of stylized trees.
How I love this upstart marriage of East and West.

The aria reaches its zenith when I enter
Booth #23, a dark cove devoted to things Nippon:
The era before Pearl Harbor,

Before the high society ladies scratched off
Nippon from the bottom of tea sets
Delicate and filigreed as small, old hands.

The aria reaches its zenith, which
Would have been enough to fog my glasses,
Enough to flood my eyes. But

There on the wall a strange painting
Startles me. It is so topsy-turvy, so unidealized
I have to get closer to it to see what gives.

A cacophony of bird wings, helter-skelter
 Like a firestorm, in faded red and muddy
Charcoal. Birds adrift like autumn leaves.

It reads: Sparrows Falling from the Sky.
Hiroshima. Circa 1900. Artist Unknown.
It grips me by the throat—rain on my face.

Only Africa Listens

Greg Moglia

One last batch remains of the drug that treats African sleeping
    sickness
Enough for one thousand victims and it doesn't pay to make any
    more

Africa has three hundred thousand infected and a blockbuster drug
Can make a billion dollars but you need buyers

The tsetse fly injects its saliva with a parasite that enters the brain
First, I hallucinate, then shout all night long

Later, a touch to my skin and I scream
Then a coma

Somewhere in Africa there's a woman with a baby
She's coming to water - to the home of the fly

In the U.S. that's me teaching mostly white children
To be kind to the poor and help whenever you can

I wonder should I say to stay alive, gain a sickness you can pay for
And let none of your children be born in Africa

Become a success in your world but never breathe Africa
Watch on television then turn away

Karl Marx's wife once dreamt that he had lost both his hands
Suddenly, she became indispensable to him

Someday Africa
You will have our hands

Strange Fruit

James Gage

We refuse to see that we will not see,
and that keeps us safely from guilt.

Ask the station-man, the utility man, the man
in the cell block. Ask the master of the Humvee,
but he won't recognize either
this need that defines your disorder:
the blight of the first world
that rips flesh from the third.

So drink up your martini
and suck dry the fruit,
slip the noose around the neck of the natives
and strip the bark clean—

thatch hut torched and the naked cheek turned;
reap and then reap and then reap and then burn.

Living in Different Worlds

"And if all I know how to do is speak, it is for you I shall speak".
Aimé Césaire

Gregory Gilbert Gumbs

Yes, I understand that for you, Northern tourists, who see
and are fascinated
by the endless white sands
embracing the beautiful blue seas
By the nearly cloudless blue skies
giving way to painterly moonlit nights

Yes, I understand that you who view
my small Caribbean Island from the comfort of your air-condi-
tioned
hotel window
or the closed window of a local taxi-cab
or a huge foreign-owned and operated touring bus
overflowing with sweet and empty calypso and reggae songs
No, not roots reggae or in-your-face calypso music, for
In these Islands, the Northern tourists are always the Kings and
Queens, you know
Yes, I understand that you do and
Cannot see and grasp
The anger and pride of the poorly paid servants
whom you and the local hotel managers condemn as being
incredibly rude
Yes, I understand that you
Cannot see and grasp
The ugly and unending poverty just a few streets away from
where you are staying
in your luxurious hotel overflowing with all of the latest
amenities
which those same rude people serving you cannot afford
Yes, I understand that you

Cannot see and grasp
The ongoing struggle of the overwhelming majority of the people
 for
Better living conditions in these so-called island paradises
Yes, I understand that you
will not see and learn to appreciate
The pounding, pounding, pounding of the restless Caribbean Sea
 against the wonderfully rocky and sharp Northern shores of the
 little Island
Slowly, wearing them down bit by bit
Which you never visit because there is no white sand beach there

Yes, I understand that for you
this is merely Uncle Sam's backyard
Far removed from your monotonous and more and more
 mechanized and artificial
Northern lifestyles
Your Idea of Paradise Lost for as long as it lasts
Even if by chance you happen to bump into the poverty and
 the misery
of the natives hidden away in back street alleys by the
overeager local authorities dedicated to pleasing you and only
 you
Yes, I understand that
for you this is all just sheer exoticism
Colourful and inevitable as the sun or the painterly moonlit night
 or
A Haitian painting
which you view in passing without taking the time to fully
 comprehend

Maybe, even buy, to brighten up your dull Northern living room
 walls
with these painters' bold and fierce ballet of colors
But, for me, you see
This is my home, mi patria, mein heimat, mon pays, mijn eiland

169

And the angry, exhausted and rude servants and the poor people
    and local artists
You see, these people are
My people, mon gens, mijn mensen, mi gente
And I,
 I, you see
Cannot fail to see
The other side of paradise.

Metro Transit 16

Diana Fu

> *"You irritating poodle, choke ya ass til ya blue*
> *or some Chinese noodles, splatter ya brains like goo*
> *They rolled out the yellow tape for the side-walk*
> *Forensics outlined ya body with the white chalk*
> *Neighbors asking, "Who done it, who did it?"*
> *Ah, just forget it! Mouth shouldn't have shitted…"*

It's hard to capture rhythm on paper, but boy, they had rhythm alright. The black kids, the ones who slouched in packs, smoked their imaginary pipes, and bounced to some unheard music bursting through their limbs and written on their ever-spread hands. They bounced always in the back of the Metro Transit bus. They spit out half sentences as if they owned the whole damned stretch of seats in front, owned our attention because they did not own the world outside. Their rhythm was contagious.

Aunt Rosanna was pissed. I could tell because of the annoyed way she was fanning herself with section A of *The New York Times* and because she had actually shoved her ass onto my part of the seat so she could turn to face the dirty windows instead of me. I wanted to tell her how awful she looked with her stringy, oiled, graying hair clinging like an octopus to her washboard back and her small breasts protruding at two points like a starved cow's tits, how she was as superstitious as a Chinese country bumpkin sometimes, and that she should stop smacking her flat face into my dim life. I itched to remind her that, after all, I was skipping an entire afternoon of ecstatic idleness to accompany her to the cheap Chinese dentist in St. Paul and that I was ready to jump the MT-16 if she kept on feeding me that sickening halfway glance.

She kept sniffling her nose like she caught some God-awful cold in mid-June. She looked somehow weaker these days. The white around her pupils had become less distinct. Her half-assed glances, the heat, and the noise all kind of ticked me off. I could tell

Aunt Rosanna wanted me to ask her what was wrong. It also ticked me off that she always spent a lot of time *hinting* things. So I resolved to silence as my defense. It worked.

"So, what did you do about Steve?"

"Huh?" I pretended not to know who Steve was although I had been swapping mouth germs with him the day before in the park.

"That idle boy who draws black cats. You haven't had sex with him, have you?" Her tone was almost urgent.

"Steve's not idle and he doesn't *draw*. He paints. And the only time he's ever painted a black cat just happened to be in the background of the only work you bothered to look at."

"If he wasn't so idle, he'd be in school right now studying biochemistry instead of smoking in parks at night and drawing those silly cats."

"It was an abandoned animal. Steve took pity on the poor thing and took him in for a portrait, probably the only one that cat's ever going to have in his life. Steve has compassion."

"Trust me, Mary, a guy with compassion isn't going to pull through in life. A guy with a job is. Now's your chance to cut if off. Auntie's not going to wait for the day he sucks you clean and takes off."

"I'm not going to dump him just because I got into college. I love him, okay? I know that must be foreign to you." I realized the words were too sharp before I finished saying them. But they came out anyway. And they hurt her.

Aunt Rosanna turned to face the windows again. After she seduced Professor Dickinson to get my dad a graduate teaching position in the States, she never dated again. That was almost ten years ago. It made me feel guilty. I knew too well (and she reminded me often) that I owe my being here and everything "American" about me to her efforts. Hell, people would have still been butchering my Chinese name, "Xi Xiaoli" if Aunt Rosanna hadn't gotten it fixed up as Mary Xi awhile back. She fixed up everybody's name in our family when we landed in the U.S. ten years ago so that we became descendants of dead British Royalties: Baba went from "Xi

Dali" to "Henry Xi" and Mama from "Xi Chuan" to Elizabeth Xi."
Ever since then, I've dreaded all public announcements of our
family. Once, when we went to Immigration and Naturalization
Services together, they had to page the whole British lineage, "Will
Henry XI, Elizabeth XI and Mary XI please step forward to claim
your passports?" Old King Henry must have cried in his grave
knowing that a small-boned, five foot five son of a Chinese counter-
revolutionary was named after him. But like always, Aunt Rosanna
made the judgment call, "If you and a white person were both
equally qualified for a job, they're going to take the one with the
English name."

******

Aunt Rosanna didn't like riding the Metro Transit 16. She
said it unnerved her. She wasn't the only one intimidated by this
bus. MT-16 had a reputation. Just what it is, I am not so sure. I first
heard the rumor from the unshaven guys who huddled, snickered,
and lingered in loose circles of smoke in a hole sunken into the side
of Brooks Hall. You could never tell if they were pretending to be
criminals or if they were serenading in the moonlight, blowing that
white spirit into each other's mouths so they could all catch lung
cancer. They often puffed about the MT-16. "Yea, you ever been on
the thing, man? That bus is like the shrine circus. It's wicked, man.
You got your hobos singing about their dogs, your illegal Mexican
immigrants, your Asian mamas, and the niggers in the back, singing
their shit." Then, five days in a row last fall, I came upon the same
odd, idling couple smoking and gulping mournful cups of air
midway on the Washington Avenue Bridge. Their flat silhouettes
touched heads intimately as they whispered about the ship of the
DDD—demented, decrepit, and destitute. Long after the incident,
which still gives me the jitters, rumors about MT-16 kept piling up
until I didn't know whether to think of it as a bus or an asylum, a
shelter, or just an old train for people who slouched their whole
lives away.

But one thing was for certain: MT-16 was definitely colored.
And I mean that in a very biological sense. There were the silent,
tired Hispanic working men, the Hmong ladies who strap every-

thing-groceries and babies alike-in a blanket on their tired backs, the few specks of retired whites and college students, and the hordes of noisy black people at the back singing the most powerful chords in the silence. This odd mixture of people had only two things in common: they were all crushed in one form or another onto a bus that refused to be categorized and they were all headed to downtown Saint Paul. It was a sweaty Monday afternoon. The sun was killing me.

******

The interior of the MT-16 didn't seem any different from other metro buses I'd been on—the same blue patterned, hard seats that craved for padding, the Nicorette ads, rope handles hanging from top bars that I never could reach, and the faint smell of summer stench. The bus was unusually crowded for a Sunday afternoon. A lanky, pimple faced punk kid stood two feet away from us. His yellow and black Mohawk weighed down on his birdlike head, which, at the moment, was bobbing up and down to his headphone music. "Burn those mother fuckers…burn those mother fucking son-of-a bitches…" he kept to the beat. He wore a torn black shirt with two devilish eyes and the white print words, "The System."

The black kids at the back of the bus had started to snicker, spit, and smack their thighs like a tropical band. I hadn't noticed when we climbed on, but boy, did they change up the mundane atmosphere with their colorful, addictive beat. But somehow, their words faltered as they drifted towards the front of the bus, faltered in my ears like a poorly written composition. The tall guy with the gleaming black face started rapping something about a Chinese chop as he rocked his broad, muscle-packed body back and forth, slicing the air into treble and bass clefs with his spread out hands. I know what the old mainlanders would have said in between cracking roasted sunflower seeds and imported dragon eye fruits. They would have called rapping a criminal act, the first step into falling off from the Harvard track and into the gutters with all the rest of the street musicians, modern artists, poets, and dirty, good-for-nothing rats. The only person who seemed to be enjoying the rap was the jovial bus driver mouthing the words along with his generous brown lips.

******

The rap started to get real loud now. Two other boys closed their hands around their mouths and hunched over as if they were heating their frigid bodies in front of a fire in the dead of winter. The resulting sound was a tremendously powerful bass that accompanied the main "melody" like some punk's stereo on the second floor. And then the percussion: five smaller boys slapping their legs and the rhythm bouncing like beads from their jerking frames. It knocked the silence out of the windows, crashing into the streets, and rolling down a string of cacophonous honking below. They swayed to a rhythm that would grow mute in a concert hall, an organ in itself that made the detached people cringe at the sound of blood pouring through the veins of the living. It was all so deafening. I was captivated. Aunt Rosanna was not amused. She stopped fanning herself and started to make short grunting sounds of disapproval. The eldest one with vigorously shining black skin scrutinized Aunt Rosanna carelessly underneath his cream-colored beret, as if he understood her Chinese. Then, with a slight nod to his gang, he gave the signal that once again punctured the thin silence with staccato beats that were as alive and as essential as the hot blood running through their chests. The invisible rhythm synchronized their movements, bounced to their hands, their heads, and their beings.

Aunt Rosanna, feeling a little hurt by their silent insult, searched for an empathetic ear and found it in a respectable looking old lady sitting right across from us. She tilted across the narrow aisle and said, "Kids these days, so rude. They need some good spanking, teach them to respect their elders."

"Oh yes, I'm telling you," replied the respectable lady. "It's this kind of foul language that's corrupting today's youth. I caught my granddaughter listening to this rap thing one time and I told her, 'Elsie, this is not music. Grandma has learned to tolerate Britney Spears but I cannot allow you to ruin your ears and lose your soul listening to that kind of foul language.' It's just immoral, that's what." Her lips were so thin that if it wasn't for the meticulously applied pink lipstick, you might have missed it altogether. The only thing that made you question her respectability was her feet. They were big, swollen, glaringly white, with veins laced in by her sandal straps, kind of like stringed up chicken breasts at the grocery store.

"Yes. Absolutely immoral," Aunt Rosanna echoed. "When I was their age in China, I was sent to the countryside to work and spent every night listening to the illegal English radio channel. Now that's how you learn correct English grammar." This affirmation brightened the respectable lady's spirits and she continued with an energized voice,

"I'm telling you, all this rap thing is good for is fostering violence and gangs and the next thing you know, young people are driving airplanes into buildings. If I were *their* parents (here, she tilted her head emphatically at the black kids), I'd teach them the right manners. That's just the sad state in today's society. As elders in the community, we've got to look after these poor kids and shield them from these types of corruptin' music."

"That's right. When I was a kid during the culture revolution, we had to salute to Chairman Mao and bow to our elders." Aunt Rosanna chimed.

"Well of course," continued the respectable lady as if she knew all about what Chinese kids did in the 70's. "And that's exactly why I've spent a good thirty years of my life tutoring inner city kids in Minneapolis. I'm telling you, it's such a burden sometimes and often I've wanted to quit. But I just keep praying to God and reminding myself that Jesus always helped the less fortunate."

"Oh yes, God has been good. When I first came, it was the Jehovah's Witnesses who took me into their homes and taught me English vocabulary from the Bible. I used to think Buddha got me here but now I realize, it was Jesus all along that helped me survive in my new country. For Christ sake, Jesus taught me English grammar. But some kids, they grow up with gold surrounding them but they throw it all away and rob the rest of us of our honest money. Personally, I don't know why Jesus brought *them* here in the first place," Aunt Rosanna declared boldly.

At this comment, a chubby salesman suddenly straightened

up and cleared his throat, "Well, now, I ought to disagree with that. Jesus didn't *bring* nobody here. It was the darn slave owners back then in the South that shipped them here."

He was sitting a few seats away from us. On his generous lap lay a weather worn briefcase. His few strands of greasy hair was brushed authoritatively to the right side of his head and when he spoke, he'd pat the briefcase occasionally as if it contained some important files. He had the look of someone who was not used to wearing a blazer, someone who had gotten shuffled into one of the tall glass buildings in downtown Minneapolis by accident. He pulled at the corners of his blazer and continued,

"Speaking as a good, honest American, I can say that as proud as I am of our country, we did do some pretty shameful things in the past. I mean, slavery was downright cruel, and I condemn it wholeheartedly. But all I'm saying is that some people need to move on. History is history. In these days, everyone with a good head on their shoulders and some sense left has a good shot at getting a hand in the stock market. It's like what I tell my kids, you gotta quit whining and get to work. The world's not going to stop for you. If I can make it coming from rural Minnesota, then any man can pull themselves up by their bootstraps too."

Then, as if to reassure himself that he'd actually made it, he patted his briefcase again and straightened his blazer with renewed confidence. By this time, most passengers had caught the drift of the conversation and were listening with an interested air except for a tired Hispanic woman holding a baby on her lap who dozed off. Even the jovial bus driver had assumed a serious expression and cocked his curly black head.

A shy college student in the front of the bus made a sudden movement with his book and started to spout with usual urgency, "Yea, sir. I'm totally with you on that. I mean, it's about equal opportunity, right? The real culprit is today's race conscious society. What I mean is, it's no longer about equal opportunity. It's about preferential treatment for minorities simply because of their skin color. When I see my friend, I don't see his skin color. I see that he likes Eminem, goes to the same bars as me, and can debate politics.

The thing people can't seem to grasp is that as the income gap widens in our society, race is nothing compared to class. I mean, there's just too many kids on the streets and it doesn't matter if they're white or black. They're poor and that's the bottom line," the college boy finished bravely and then slumped down once again in this corner as if the words drained him.

"Haha, well said, son. It's kids like you who are going to change the way the world spins," declared the chubby salesman, again with the air of stolen authority.

"Yes, thank goodness there's still some sense in *certain* young folks," added the respectable lady as she looked back piercingly at the black kids and then exchanged knowing glances with Aunt Rosanna. And then, as if noticing me for the first time, she asked, "and what does this darling young lady do?"

"I don't *do* anything. I'm not a *doing* kind of person." I smiled angelically. Aunt Rosanna poked me on the side and answered for me, "She's a freshman at the University, an honors student. She's been on the Dean's list two semesters in a row. We wanted her to go to Harvard, of course, but since she got a full scholarship at the University, we let her just stay in Minnesota for her undergrad."

"I got rejected from Harvard," I said flatly. That really pissed Aunt Rosanna off, and the old lady, sensing the bubbling discomfort, tactfully changed the subject, "Well, at least she's grateful for what this country can provide. You should be proud of her. And anyway, there's enough Chinese in those Ivy Leagues already, right? How bout some diversity at the state schools?" She laughed heartedly at her own joke. Her double chin jiggled jovially. Then she moved as if she was going to stroke my hair. I pulled my head back instinctively.

"Oh yes," she continued, refusing to notice my disgust. "At least she ain't like *some* kids who don't know the difference between a gun and a pencil and who run around this beautiful country spreadin' all sorts of violence."

Before she could rattle on any further, the bus suddenly veered sideways so violently that my knees hit the back of the seats in front of us and the people standing were tossed towards then front of the bus. The rope handles swung jerkily and one of the Nicorette ads popped out of its plastic display case, floating to the floor. The people were screaming and scrambling in every direction to gather their possessions. The respectable lady's feather hat had flown off as she tried to take charge, "Duck down, everyone! There's been a terrorist attack!" The chubby salesman ignored her as he elbowed anyone who got in the way of his chase for the paper-work that had burst from his flopped open briefcase. The college student was curled in his seat and looked lost.

Amid the commotion, I caught sight of Aunt Rosanna. At the collision, she was thrown backwards and had unfortunately landed in a bony heap right in the middle of the black rappers.

"Help me! Mary! Come here, quick."

She sounded as if she was being raped. Her face had been drained of color and seemed like a sheet of yellow wax paper. She was shivering. Just then a black hand reached under her bony elbow and pulled her up. Aunt Rosanna screamed, ran forward, and charged right into the white punk kid.

In a moment of delirium, I don't know if Aunt Rosanna had lost her vision or her mind. She started pounding the tall punk kid's stomach with her shriveled fists as if he was a brick wall she had to break through. Except this one didn't give in to her clawing. She was pounding him as if someone had been dancing on her life string, making it snap. "Black ghosts, black ghosts," she kept on saying over and over again in Chinese until the whole bus rocked with silence, like a sleeper swinging in a hammock under the trees.

She caught him so off guard that he just stood still for a few moments, watching the five foot three Chinese woman box her way through his tight abdomen. Then he came to his senses. With a quick fling of the arm, he pushed his attacker off.

"Mother fucking chink come back from hell!"

That was it. That's all he said. Sheer profanity. A curse. Aunt Rosanna became calm suddenly. She just stood there firmly with her sticky gray hair blowing from the wind that flew in from the windows and clutched tightly onto the handle bars above with

179

her skinny arms, stretched as tall as any southern Chinese woman could be. She looked so frail in her thin red silk dress that stuck to her skeletal frame. The 24karat miniature Jesus Christ around her wrinkled neck outshone the sun. Her yellowish skin looked transparent, almost revealing the worms crawling just beneath the surface. I don't know how long she stood like that, solemnly awaiting what she knew was coming.

When the bus had snaked around Washington, the liquid red sun had fallen in a heap, and the smoke from the Spaghetti factory rose like embers that sizzled off of baking yams on West Nanjing Street.

"Wo, folks. Sorry about that disturbance. There was a boulder on the road and I didn't wanna run it over. No need to sweat it. We'll be at Nicollet Mall in no time," the bus driver announced casually.

******

It was not until the day Aunt Rosanna passed away a few months later that I figured out why the bus driver's big dark eyes twinkled with an unnatural light that day. I caught him chuckling mischievously, his black skin almost burned under the sunlight. I remembered how he slowly combed his curly hair in the rearview mirror and waved goodbye to all the battered folks who staggered off the MT-16.

That day on the bus didn't do much for Aunt Rosanna's frail health condition. For weeks afterwards, she kept saying how she heard from God that morning about the chained people who would never make it because they didn't know how to taste the fruit that was given to them, that only people who were going into the soil knew not to struggle for things that had no meaning.

******

The air was as hot and humid as a dusty Nanjing in August when Aunt Rosanna passed away. She'd known it all along that the worms were eating away at her flesh from the inside and that the soil couched more dead corpses than it did living plant bulbs. She wanted to see the cheap Chinese dentist one more time so he could fix her teeth just right because they were the last remnants of her after everything else eroded into the streams in circles of dusty sediments. After that, we went and sat on the stone bench at the tiny little park in St. Paul where all the dirty pigeons lived; it was the first place she took me when I came to the U.S. ten years ago. She asked if the pigeons still frightened me like they did when I was younger, told me that I was the smartest little kid she knew because I could name all the animals at the Nanjing City Zoo when she used to peddle me on the backseat of her bicycle in China, and that she hoped I would come to my senses about Steve and marry a white Harvard academic when I got out of college.

"I'm not saying Steve's a bad guy, Mary. It's just that sometimes it helps when your husband actually fixes the toilet instead of admiring how it shines under a certain lighting."

Then, after a long, almost solemn pause, she suddenly asked me if I thought there was a boulder that day on the route of the MT-16. "Who's ever heard of a boulder on the middle of the downtown road, Mary? If there was one, then I don't know what state government has been doing all these years. There was no boulder, right?"

Aunt Rosanna left on one of those summer nights right after a thunderstorm, when the dark, mushy soil cradled century-old droplets of sweat left by those who tilled the land and built the houses.

In Dostoyevsky's Atmosphere

Annie Dawid

1980
Leningrad / St. Petersburg

Turning the corner off the Nevsky Prospect, Freda and Berthold hold hands, two old siblings on what may be the last voyage for both — who can say? Six months ago she was diagnosed with early Parkinson's disease, and Berthold last year suffered his third heart attack since his wife's death on their return from America. Hence, the grand *tour du monde*.

"Pity, a pity I will never understand," says Berthold, pointing to the decaying buildings, masonry crumbling from once ornate balconies and cornices as they walk in the direction of Dostoyevsky's home, now a museum. Literature has always been Freda's passion, and in every city they visit, she steers them toward the places where the great books in her library were written.

"Yes. It could have been Paris — all its charm squandered, its grandeur stuffed into the ugly mold of Stalin." She dreams of home, her oak-lined street beside the Luxembourg Gardens, the civilized French culture she had adopted as her own, five decades previously.

"You were lucky, dear Freda, never to live in a Communist country. I thank the god I don't believe in that you and Bebe were spared."

They look in a butcher's window at a spindly-looking chicken alone on its shelf, and a slab of bacon, a sickly grayish color — the only merchandise displayed. A line of babushka-covered women curves like a scimitar out the door and around the block. The women hurl insults at the butcher, who can't hear them for the din, and at one another. Freda's rudimentary knowledge of Russian and her good eyes tell her these women lead hard lives, lives in which buying a passable piece of meat for their family's dinner marks a profound accomplishment.

"Even in the worst days of the war," Freda murmurs as they

pass the last woman in line, "we were never this hopeless."

"Because you knew it was going to end." Berthold stops to rest, leaning against a street sign. There are few benches in St. Petersburg; those they see crumble like the buildings, useless.

Freda offers her cane. "Take this. I'm feeling very strong today."

Berthold has lost his hair in addition to his healthy girth. And his once formidable height has diminished too, as he stoops while walking, sitting or standing. At times, she can hardly bear to look at him — her big, powerful brother, who always thrived no matter the circumstances. Broken. She herself will never break, she thinks.

Accepting the cane, he winks. "My baby sister with a degenerative disease offers her walking stick to the weak-hearted old brother. Freda, has it come to this?"

She kisses his cheek, which feels like paper, dry and stiff. "You'll see: when we get to the great writer's house, we will be rejuvenated. He knew the souls of men. Just to breathe the air in his home will make you better."

Suddenly, a dozen children, holding hands, emerge from an alley. Cheeks bright with cold, they sing as their teacher leads them across the street. The last little boy, perhaps five years old, turns to wave. The teacher yells at him to hurry up. Berthold and Freda wave back.

"What were they singing?" he asks, straightening up and offering his right arm, which she takes, his left clutching the cane. They cross the street, and, without waiting for her answer, Berthold adds: "The children, thank god, will thrive if they have their parents' love. Communism means nothing to them yet."

"This misery," Freda says, pointing to the once-white blackened walls, an overflowing garbage can, windows cracked and partly blocked with cardboard, "is it any different than the misery under the Czar?" A very old woman whose shoes are wound with tape, trailing behind her like a tail, trudges by on the other side of the street. "I wouldn't want to grow old here."

"Yes," Berthold says, following her gaze. "Poor Papa. If

only he'd lived a little longer, he could have died with Mama in freedom."

"Was he broken, do you think? I mean, to have known such success as a young man, and to die with so little...." She doesn't expect an answer, as she and her siblings have discussed their father's end so many times, always trying to frame it in hopeful terms: he was surrounded by his family, his sturdy grandchildren, they had enough to eat. Yet now, she wonders, as her own mortality looms, is it worth pretending? Men are weaker than women, she tells herself, bent more easily by life.

"Broken!" Berthold stands up straighter and turns her face toward his. "Papa was never broken! Broke, maybe." He laughs. "Remember the Dresden Bank failure? But what did he do? He took us to a better place." Berthold sighs and lets go, seeing Freda's lips pursed as if in disapproval. "At *that* time, it was. Who could have foreseen the war and everything that followed?"

"When I think about it now," she says thoughtfully, staring at the back of the tiny old woman as she disappears from view, "I can see only irony. Everyone went West, while Papa took us East."

"That was his genius! Not to follow the crowd." Berthold looks around. "So, where is your beloved writer's home? I thought you said it was on this corner."

Freda looks for a sign announcing the writer's dwelling but sees nothing. It is an ordinary street corner, drab to the point of despair — appropriate, she thinks, for the creator of Raskolnikov. "Perhaps it isn't marked."

"Yes. I remember that about the Communist years in Rumania, how certain artists could be declared for the State or against it. Even if they were dead before the State ever existed!" He wipes his eyes with a handkerchief. "Have I remembered to tell you this week or this month or this year how wonderful you are for having rescued me?"

She waves him off. "Berthold, you have thanked me a hundred times, a thousand times. You would have done it for me."

"But one is useless in prison. I couldn't help anyone. Sometimes now I wonder if Hans was right, if I should have stayed in England, if I could have gotten *all* the family out from there, and sooner." He sighs, loudly. "I'm tired. Can we go back to the hotel?"

"Don't be a revisionist, Berthold. It doesn't help. You did what you thought was right. We can all look back now and say we should have done things differently. I try not to. When I question Papa's choices I ask myself if I am a hypocrite if I fail to question myself. We were lucky, you know, me and Pierrot and Charles and Bebe in Aix. And how I dared to have another child!" She shakes her head. "I thought I was so very clever, but I was just lucky."

"We were all lucky, *ma chérie*." He leans against the building, panting hard. "Not so for our cousins in Dresden. You must promise me to take care of Anna, in England, after I'm gone."

Freda doesn't answer, as she has heard this request many times since his first heart attack. She is scanning the other corners, now, for a sign. Although it is only September, the wind here feels like winter, and the light goes early.

"Promise me!"

"Berthold, of course. But I don't like to speak as if your death is imminent. You may live a long time yet. Perhaps we'll take another around-the-world-in-80-days tour!" She cannot really contemplate a life without her brother. Pierrot had died so young she had formed her identity as a widow. But her siblings, they endured and endured. When Berthold speaks to her of Anna, she hears only the sound of death talking. But he has already lived through three heart attacks; surely he will outlive her own fatal illness.

Just as she is about to conclude either the hotel clerk's directions were wrong, or else Dostoyevsky is out of fashion, she spies in the dirty window of what appears to be a small apartment, a small, hand-lettered sign in Cyrillic: The Dostoyevsky Museum. No hours are listed, but an arrow points toward a narrow doorway. Gray paint flakes from the lintel, black cobwebs line the corners, and trash piles in front of the door. Nevertheless, she knocks.

Berthold shakes his head. "The great writer has been consigned to the ghetto! And no one is home. Let's go, *chérie*."

Freda feels defeated. What might redeem this sad city for

her has been denied. Even the Hermitage was depressing, reinforcing the cold, the neglect, the darkness of these poor people's lives, even with their great collection of decaying art. Yet words, she believes, are the highest form of art. She would never say this aloud to her sisters with their fierce dedication to music above all. Berthold with his paintings, his love of the painted tableau; she shares these affinities, but for Freda, text reigns supreme, for it doesn't need an expert interpreter to summon it anew, or a special climate free from moisture or aridity to preserve its greatness. It needs only a reader, someone like her or like any of these St. Petersburgers (she hates to say Leningrad) with none of the pleasures money has bought Freda — her travels to Tahiti, New Zealand, New York, London, Tokyo. Of course she relishes such pleasures, enjoys them especially now that her mobility is endangered. But to sit home with a good book…. If her disease should prevent her from reading, Freda thinks, she will die.

Sighing, she turns to follow Berthold back the way they had come. From behind, a young man taps her on the shoulder. Wearing thick glasses and a threadbare jacket, he says something with the word Dostoyevsky in it in the form of a question with an accompanying raised eyebrow and rising intonation.

"*Da. Dostoyevsky doma, pajalusta,* " Freda manages in return.

Taking her elbow, he steers Freda, pulling Berthold in tow, toward another door around the corner, unmarked and untended. As if revealing contraband, he pulls a silver skeleton key from his pants pocket. Freda wonders if she should offer money, and how much, and then what kind of currency would be most helpful to him, but as she fumbles to open her purse, the man closes his hand over hers.

"This way," he says in English.

Inside they find a dim hallway leading to a flight of stairs. Slowly, pausing to breathe on each step, Berthold and Freda ascend.

At the top, the man unlocks another door, lights a kerosene lamp, and they step into another century, a rich universe of wooden bookcases crammed with volumes, finely appointed furniture so foreign to the dingy world on the other side of the door.

"My mother, she is caretaker. I come to study at night, but I cannot turn lights on. I must leave curtains closed." Even the young man seems different inside — somehow lighter, not quite the starving student he'd appeared earlier, perhaps a man of letters. In his hand, Freda now notices, he carries a copy of *The Brothers Karamazov.* She envies him his youth, its possibilities, a writer studying one of the greatest writers of all in his very own *study.*

"You also write?" she asks in English, not trusting her Russian to carry her in conversation.

He smiles, pointing to the desk on which he has now lit a candle. On its surface are tiny spectacles, crossed underneath, as if left yesterday by Dostoyevsky himself. There are papers half-covered with script scattered around, a pen, an inkwell, a photograph of what must be his parents.

"Here I write, in a small notebook, without disturbing his tools." He pulls a small black notebook from his back pocket and offers it to Freda.

Berthold has seated himself in an armchair by the door and appears to be dozing. This is their established pattern in the cities they'd visited: she enraptured in writers' homes, he nodding off, while in museums he was the expert, offering art history which sometimes bored her, so that often she found her way to the café and sat. It worked beautifully, their complementary loves.

"What is it you write?" She dares to open the cover, revealing neat Cyrillic script, graceful penmanship waltzing across the unlined pages. She feels sure it is something potent, magical. A reader since early childhood, Freda had never written, envying those who dared. "A novel?"

The man pulls out the desk chair, a highly polished mahogany upholstered armchair, and tells her to sit. "Pajalusta."

Flushing with pleasure, Freda sits. "Das svedania."

"I shall answer your question," says the man, leaning against the desk after making sure he won't alter the writerly tableau on its surface. "No, I am no novelist. Someday, perhaps. I write what I see. How you call it? Not-fiction."

"A historian of your times. A documentarist."

Puzzled, he pulls a smaller notebook from his breast pocket and begins to write. "Docu-*shto*?"

Freda runs her fingertip along the desktop. No dust, no decay here. She feels something powerful sitting in this seat, something stirring as she touches the long black fountain pen, resting on a glass holder as if waiting for the next thought, the next word.

"Documentary writer. Like a filmmaker." She wonders if they will have any references in common. "Like Ophuls' *The Sorrow and the Pity*."

He shakes his head. "I do not know this."

"Perhaps I make a distinction that is not necessary." She points to *The Brothers Karamazov*. "Here, too, Dostoyevsky records his times, his moment in history, yes?"

The man nods. "Yes of course. But he tells a lie, he invents. There were no brothers Karamazov, only visions in his head."

"Yes. Beautiful lies, though. Magnificent visions. This is art, yes?"

He places his own notebook on the table. "My writing, I think, is not art."

She passes her fingertips over his pages, leafs through the script so sculpted and lovely its very letters seem art itself. "You are young."

He shrugs. "Not so very young. By my age, Dostoyevsky already wrote great works. Me, not so. I am not a genius."

She pats his hand. "You don't have to be a genius to make art. Don't rush. You have plenty of time."

He looks at his watch. "Excuse me, but we must go now."

Freda looks back at Berthold, now snoring. The shadowy room pulses with spirit, not only the dead writer's but the young man's as well, and perhaps something of her own, kindling inside her, shines in the reflection of the candle on the fine-grained mahogany desk.

"Of course. You have made my trip to St. Petersburg complete. Please let me give you something." In her wallet she finds a twenty-dollar bill, what's left of their Boston cash. "Please, take this. To buy your next notebook, perhaps."

"A new pen," says the man, "I will buy a fabulous fountain pen on the black market that doesn't leak, and then I will write here, my ink drying in Dostoyevsky's atmosphere."

"Yes."

With difficulty, Freda rises. Her legs feel stiff; now she needs her cane. With the young man at her side, she manages to awaken her brother, and, together, they descend slowly the narrow stairs and make their way to the street, where dusk envelops them.

Southern California Missionaries in the Holy Land

David Starkey

At first, they seemed amused
by our bleached hair and surfer-
speak, almost sympathetic. But
that didn't last. Too much anger
sifting among the dust and smog.
I thought it was thunder, the first time
I heard a Cobra helicopter's guns.

Guns everywhere. Machinegun
poking from an elementary
school, masked gunmen in leather
jackets and jeans. Brad and I
would duck down
the fetid alleys at the sound,
always startling, of gunfire.

I remember two soldiers smoking
atop their tank. Blood-soaked
bandages around a woman's neck
and arms. Politicians in blue suits
and silk ties. A body growing
stiff under a white sheet.
Memories for ten years now.

To my certain knowledge,
we didn't save a single soul
in all our wanderings amid the water
towers and stones, amid the smoke
rising from refugee camps, mosques
and synagogues. Our Bibles
became dense with marginalia.

Bloodlines

Carol Bergman

My friend, Nabila, an Israeli Arab by birth and an American citizen by choice, wrote me an email the other day thanking me for my commitment to justice and a better world. High praise from my friend, a professor at Columbia University who does much more than I—traveling to faraway places on Soros Foundation Grants to set up HIV prevention programs, for example. Nonetheless, it is heartwarming, unexpected and humbling in a friendship such as ours.

What did I do? Not very much. I had been to an inspirational weekend at the Omega Institute and heard Christopher Reeve, Anna Quindlen, and Robert Kennedy Jr. speak. This was a 60th birthday present to myself, an attempt to recharge after finishing the publicity for "Another Day in Paradise," a compilation of stories by international humanitarian workers I compiled and edited. Two-thirds of the book is about war and I wasn't feeling very optimistic by the time I finished. So I went along to the conference. In between two of the keynote speakers, I took a workshop called "The Natural Singer," offered by Claude Stein. There were sixty people in the room, mostly women. Within minutes we were singing to each other in bold on-key voices. My partner was Meredith who had traveled down from Ithaca for the occasion. I liked her fresh, make-up free face and rough hands. I thought she must be a gardener, which she was. Later I also learned she is a baker.

We looked into each other's eyes as Claude created melodies on his keyboard and told us what to sing, all new-agey stuff such as, "I have the right to be here singing to you. My voice is strong. I am so beautiful." Pretty soppy. Nonetheless, I started sobbing.

Though tears come easily to me, I felt exposed, and embarrassed. I'd had a hard few days and was feeling sad about my aging mother and some wrong turns with my husband, Jim. It all fell out of me. So hard was I crying that I couldn't pay attention to Meredith and her sorrows and hopes, musically rendered. This was the lesson, in fact, and one I have thought about a lot since: If we only think about ourselves, our needs and personal angst, our families and clans, we cannot see other people, much less the rest of the world.

Of course, I knew all this, intellectually, when I went into the workshop. But the experience of it shocked me. Contrite, I invited Meredith and her friend Marcia, a Unitarian minister, to come with me to lunch, though I would have preferred to read. We walked a few blocks north, out of the touristy neighborhood of the hotel, to a trendy restaurant called Pain Quotidien. Sitting next to us at the communal table was John Simon, a 60 Minutes reporter, one of the best interviewers on American television. He was alone, and he looked lonely, so I didn't say anything, though I should have. In truth, I couldn't remember his name. Still, I should have said something, thanked him for being such a good reporter. Meredith recognized him too; their elbows were nearly touching. But she didn't say anything, either. As we left, we decided the encounter was a good omen, somehow, though we couldn't say in what way exactly.

By Sunday night, I was all revved up, ready to contribute something, however small, to the upcoming presidential election season, the most important in my lifetime, I decided. Christopher Reeve gave the closing speech and his presentation, personal and political, to a crowd of 400, was riveting. What a man! From him we learned many things; most importantly, to ignore despair and press on. If he can do this, we all can.

That night Nabila and her husband, Ahmad, came over for dinner. I suggested we form a support group of some kind, an antidote to the gloom we were all feeling about the Israel/Palestine conundrum. My enthusiasm was contagious and everyone agreed to organize an evening to watch a documentary about Gaza and brainstorm contributions we might make to the alleviation of the suffering there from our home base in New York. I came away with an idea to try to organize a conference of some sort at the synagogue my mother belongs to in Westport, Ct. I made contact with the rabbi, and he responded positively. This small right action, as the Buddhists say, inspired Nabila's email to me.

When we are not talking Middle East politics, the four of us—Nabila and I, Ahmad and Jim—are discussing children, food, exercise regimens, summer plans. The agonies of our ancestral homeland—my relatives live in Tel Aviv, Nabila's in a small village outside Tel Aviv, Ahmad's family on the West Bank—are an undercurrent, but they do not stop us from having fun. One day, we tell each other, we will meet in Jerusalem at an apartment Nabila recently purchased in a mixed, utopian community there. Similarly Ahmad, and Jim are planning a trip without their wives into the desert on a camel's back where they will cook a whole lamb on a spit and eat all of it without concern for cholesterol.

We could be sisters and brothers, our bloodlines commingled in an accident of history—one part Jew, one part Arab. Jim and Ahmad are jolly with slightly over-sized bellies, struggling with their weight, but enjoying every morsel they imbibe despite admonitions from their female better halves. Their happy nature balances their wives' more serious, brooding personalities. Nabila and I look alike too—with deep-set eyes, high cheekbones, Nefertiti profiles, and dark hair.

It took a while for us to meet, though we were known to each other through a mutual friend. For years, in fact, this well meaning friend, kept us apart. She was worried, she later told us, that we would argue, or worse. Having been to the Middle East herself, she assumed a blood hatred and did not want to encourage or witness it. Living as we do these days—post 9/11, post Afghanistan, post Iraq—in a culture of vengeance and war, she did not anticipate the strength of our desire for friendship and peace.

December 23

Sandy Feinstein

Three windows at my back, light too cold to feel
the day after winter begins, the swollen moon
yielding to the inevitability of rotation,

a motion uncontrolled, constant as doubt
despite decorations, bright colored bulbs
and evergreens I didn't see in Syria last year

when all three holidays converged quietly.
Traffic stopped at dusk, a drone of prayer
repeated as a feast, like Christmas.

I ate chocolates from a plastic dreidl
half remembered spinning as a child
watching candles being lit with words

that meant nothing, something about oil
and a temple, nameless was the enemy
I would later choose to keep that way.

Bad Press

Sandy Feinstein

A black vulture huddles at roadside, stray weeds
and small swirls of sand beside asphalt and rushing
cars where passengers squint at the sun and see birds
of prey, discarded black bags feathery in the light wind

like the cat napping on the window sill unnoticed,
once approached shape shifts into pink plastic
containing green peels, thin skinned limes
formerly tangerines, and wrinkled small cucumbers

unknown as countries where rumors prevail
creating weapon wielding terrorists dark as carrion
eaters and ubiquitous as fruit flies requiring
attention, yet scattered more easily than illusions.

Sunset

Sandy Feinstein

This sun takes all color with it as it sets, leaving a white backdrop
for the call that comes when it starts to go, receding into the whorl,
bleached by anticipated night, its light and heat dipping west,
where it cannot be the same, for nothing is quite the same there.

They say there are thieves and murderers, prostitutes and rapes,
neglected parents and children both, and no one walks the city
after 8:00. But they want to go anyway, bringing brides from home
who will blanch eggplants and stuff them with lamb and rice.

The sun takes winter warmth over the western edge, going
without papers, a pauper of light, showing what no one sees,
and always returning east, unassailed by marauders on either
side who shake words or worse at shadows, what's left as it sets.

The Kerchief

Beadrin Youngdahl

In Africa, a land where seven plagues would be just seven more problems, boys play. They ride bikes over their small corner of a large continent long besieged by poverty, famine, drought, and disease. Otjo, skin black but for the streaks of gray-brown where the African sun reflects light, and his friend Hans, the ranch owner's son, pale, sun creating shadow on his cheeks, share a bicycle. Otjo's legs, improbably long, pump the bike across the dusty yard while Hans, a featherweight, accepts a gleeful free ride on the handlebars. Both chatter in rapid Afrikaans, laughing in Universal Boy.

In the red plastic basket fastened to the back fender is a large tin milk can, discovered like pirates' gold near the barn at the lower ranch. The boys leap simultaneously as the bike skids to a dusty stop just short of the shed. Bare feet scramble, white ones to pull open the corrugated door, black ones to make a shuffled path with the tin, into the dark, cool space where the real fun will begin.

The milk can has a tin lid, molded to fit tightly and further secured by rust. Using a crow bar and a hammer, four scrawny and determined arms fill the late morning with sound; the chime of iron on tin and the shifting chorus of boy voices undergoing adolescent change, speculating about the contents, laughing at each other's most exciting suggestions: homemade beer, a million years old at least? They've heard legends of voodoo people out in the bush— shrunken heads or finger bones? Elephant ivory and diamonds sneaked out of mines are among the more probable suggestions. It is all banging, clanging, twisting and bending of old tin until a slip of the crow bar is followed by a gasp and a shriek.

The crow bar flips from Hans' hands and rips a bloody bite from Otjo's large, bare toe. Blood pours, red and warm, from the wound, the toenail lifted. Otjo will not cry but his face twists into a painful mask.

Hans cries out, "Mama!" and takes the kerchief from his neck—the one with which he wipes his brow, the grease from his

197

bike and catches the occasional dusty sneeze—and wraps it around
his friend's smashed toe. Otjo rocks, sitting on the dirt floor of the
shed, and makes moaning, self-comforting sounds. Hans holds the
kerchief around the toe, chewing his lower lip, not yet crying.

The mothers arrive from their separate directions. Clara,
Otjo's mother, from the laundry she is hanging in the yard; Reann
from the patio where she is taking her morning tea. Clara stoops,
rocking her son in her ample arms and cooing to him in low sounds,
she being the first not afraid to cry openly.

Reann gasps and pulls at Hans, "No. No, Hans, come here.
No."

Otjo's father, the gardener, abandons his wheelbarrow with
its load of dry leaves and twigs, speaks quickly to his wife, offers a
brief reassurance to his son, and then turns to Reann. In their
common Afrikaans language, a question, an answer, a directive,
then Reann, with a sweeping gesture, "Yes. Yes, take him. Take the
farm truck, yes, of course, to the clinic in town." She turns to her
son, tears now streaking the dust on his cheeks; she looks with
horror at the blood on his hands and commands,

"Hans, shower now. Go on."

Hans watches over his shoulder as he walks to the house.
He sees Otjo, his gangly friend, leaning on his father while climbing
with obvious pain into the farm truck, the blue, blood soaked
kerchief tied around Otjo's swollen foot.

The clinic is housed in a low, clean block building, donated,
built and maintained by charitable donors who wish to keep
poverty and illness managed well and from a distance. . Babies cry,
children sit cross-legged on the tile floor or lean against the walls,
allowing the adults and the perilously ill of the community to have
the plastic molded chairs. AIDS literature dominates the tabletops.
It is offered in various languages with lavish illustrations for those
who do not read at all. Donated condoms are freely available with
unblinking instructions on their use. The women, who glance in the
way of that garish display, avert their eyes in sincere modesty. The
staff can be seen moving around and through the clinic at a purposeful pace, bright purple Latex gloves their personal armor in a

war for which they have few real weapons. The lobby smells of antiseptic and decay. It is teeming with people seeking help. Otjo and his father wait with them, speaking in hushed tones to the neighbors they meet there. Loss is a familiar theme, Otjo's injured toe a blessing, they say. It will be fine. The doctor can fix that.

In the evening, Hans and his parents sit on the patio, dinner finished, watching the torches soften the darkness when a low, gentle voice precedes a familiar form at the patio edge.

"Missus? Good evening?" Clara approaches the patio but waits for an invitation into the light.

Reann stands and gestures, "Yes Clara. Do come. How is our Otjo? What did the doctor say?"

Clara steps onto the tile and nods a greeting to the family. Hans rises from his chair, well mannered and eager to hear of his pal, still feeling the bitter snap of the crow bar escaping his grip.

Clara graces Hans with a warm, maternal smile then speaks to Reann, "Thank you. His toe is badly hurt but the doctor used medicine and tools and dressings and repaired it well. She turns a shy smile toward Hans' father, "Like Mister with the truck some-times."

Hans' father accepts the praise with a small, proud smile.

Clara turns her attention back to Reann, "It is bandaged and still sore for him but he will heal. I thank you." She turns again to Hans and extends her hand, offering his kerchief, cleaned and ironed into a neat square, "Here Hans. Thank you for helping."

Reann reaches out in a smooth but immediate gesture. "No Hans." She says, more harshly than she may have wished. She touches Clara's hand firmly in turning it away. "No Clara. You can keep the kerchief. Hans has others. I'm glad Otjo will be well. Tell him we are thinking of him."

Clara accepts the kerchief and works its pressed edges between her fingers.

"Of course, Missus. I will tell Otjo it is a gift."

The mothers nod agreement.

Hans moves closer, "When may I see Otjo?" He seeks a response, an assurance, from either mother.

Clara and Reann both reach to gently touch the sweetness of his youthful face, both seeing the beginning of sharper, more mature edges emerging. Both smile. Clara backs away and says, from the half-light of the patio's edge, "Hans, you are a good friend to Otjo. Thank you." and, kerchief in hand, turns to face the dark path home.

The Names of Things

Cristina Perissinotto

You tourists might think that these waters
are yours, as you wrinkle your nose
or bury it in a guidebook in front of San Marco.
After all you've earned it, standing in line
for hours in the ferocious summer
to enter the *basilica* or a Murano Glass Factory.

Do not ask me the name of that church,
there are too many around here to remember
look it up in your tourist maps
or sketched journals. Our memory
is crowded with water and islands
with the numberless bridges we must climb
to find bread, meat, water to drink,
while all around is souvenirs, plastic gondolas,
masks made in Hong Kong.

We are made of fog and water, wood
and Istrian stone; our language melts in the mouth,
chirps in the morning, greets you with a word
that was invented right here, in these islands,
among these bridges, and meant: consider me
at your disposal, I am your Servant. *

* The word *ciao* comes from the Venetian *s'ciao,* which means, "I am
your slave."

Couvade

Diane Raptosh

In British Guiana, the father abstains from animal foods even before the child comes through. After birth he sips thinned gruel, cassava soup. He does not work, smoke, wash, or lay hand to weapon. He curls in his hammock, bringing pain to himself on the lips of a language no one can fathom. In Borneo after a birth, fathers start on a steady diet of salt and rice, doze far from the sun, and do not bathe for over four days. In Scotland someone might place a man's shirt on the door to protect the new baby from demons. In Baltic Europe the wife puts on her husband's shirts if he's not at home. Or his coat under her torso. His hat on her pillow. In certain parts of Prattville to this day, the husband's pants are folded and plumped under the delivering mother's back. If not his pants, then his cap. Elsewhere, the mother-to-be's grief migrates to other men or women, foxes, squirrels, pine trees, even teapot steam. A midwife might also pass the pang to the husband—laying his pants on the chopping block and splitting them with an ax: a spell thus cast. Marco Polo figured any restrictions on the man were merely a way to make him suffer as his wife did giving birth—his tit for her tat. Perhaps there's no end to the means one might use to feel one's way into the ache of another. Among the Malayans on the Molukk island Buru, the wife treats the father with delicacies while he lies in bed as though sick weeks after birth. In northern Holland the father is meant to be present to hold the mother in ways that might ease the pain, how a singer knows just what notes to maintain so the listener's left feeling held. If this didn't help, the father would go to the barn to loosen the reins of the plow: All knots untied. Reports from Vastergotland insist it is not male strength passed to the woman but masculine goodness: At times a mother-to-be called for a man of the town known to be watchful and kind. In some Alabama precincts mothers may shift their pains to the husband if he lies hip to hip by her labor. In French Guiana the father's kept in bed, cloistered, for six weeks after the baby is born. At this time family members cut holes in his skin and rub down his body with ground pepper plant. In Greenland a new dad might not work again for seven weeks. In South India, the man would have donned his wife's lightest dress, gathered some strands of her hair from a brush, and toed his slow way into the darkest room of the hut.

The Body Politic

Diane Raptosh

Male ostriches, for example, pirouette-dance only when courting other males. Gray-headed flying foxes drape wing-membranes round same-sex partners; stumptail and bonnet macaques sleep-huddle; laud all male walruses who link into extended chains, clasping each other front-to-back as they doze along sea-skin—a drowsy water-flame play zoologists tag *wuzzle.* This resembles the ways whales and dolphins drub on each other, with flippers and tail flukes. Kangaroos growl, male Anna's hummingbirds pop, male blackbuck antelopes bark, male ocellated antbirds carol, and male lions hum for the love of someone the same. The snap-hiss calls of black-crowned night herons, the croaking of male moose, the chirp-squeaks of male West Indian manatees, yip-purr calls of hammer-heads, the yelp and babble-singing of the pukeko, stutters and chirps of male cheetahs, the vacuum-slurp of male caribou and pulsive scream-calls in bowhead whales: just some of what's to be heard. Female koalas bellow, female squirrel monkeys purr, female red foxes gecker and snirk—all for the gaze of a certain girl, while musk ducks paddle-honk, plonk-sink, and whistle-kick. Even reading the word *lick* triggers blood flow where the motor cortex leads to tongue and mouth movements. And what about those pulsed sound waves male Atlantic spotted dolphins have been known to use to woo male friends? The other of the other is the same—a couple of male Bonobos out of the black-blue kissing each other so marvelously their tongues get ripped. Just now, some-where, two female hoary marmots are rubbing each others' chops; a pair of male mountain sheep are grazing each others' horns and cheeks; female galahs and orange-fronted parakeets in same-sex pairs too numerous to count are in the midst of blood-hot faux fencing bouts with their bills right as we speak. Say it with me.

V

NATURAL GIFTS

Owners of the Sky
Jeffrey J. Knowles

"Dig your fingers into the ground!" my brother, Lloyd, shouted down to me. His voice conveyed something of authority— he was six while I was a third of a lifetime behind him at four—but also something of the excitement of discovery. As with most of our fraternal wanderings through childhood he had again been the first to uncover the secret, to find the treasure, to learn the lesson.

"It's easy if you dig your fingers into the ground. You can climb right up. Watch me." I would have found his confident assertions irritating had I been anything less than terrified at that moment. I tried digging my fingers into the ground but just couldn't get the hang of it. Behind and all around me was the most unnerving and intriguing landscape this little city boy had seen. Enormous rock outcroppings jutted out over a canyon which to my fevered eyes looked four or five thousand feet deep, but actually only 30 or 40 on a direct drop. The canyon ringed the pearl of this Tolkienesk scene, a perfectly formed waterfall that tumbled into a broad, round pool below. Underneath the thrusting rock plates darkening shadows slanted back into what I was sure were deep caves. Below was the creek, splashing a winding path among a disordered array of oddly placed rocks and fallen trees. It was, I had suddenly realized, a wild world, defying sun and grass stains and mail boxes—and parental protection.

Why had we come down here anyway? Dad and Mom had strictly warned us away from this forbidding woods and waterfall just behind the property that would become our family homestead for the next half century. Yet here we were, city-boy visitors, halfway up the walls of the steep ravine that housed the dreaded place. And I was stuck, unable to go up, not daring to go down, not caring to stay put. Lloyd was saying something else from above me. I couldn't hear what he said, but did notice a dramatic change in his formerly triumphant tone. Suddenly he was no longer the authoritative older brother, but a scared little boy. Despite my predicament I lifted my nose out of the ground-hugging ferns long enough to steal a look at him. Beyond him a few feet at the top rim of the ravine, I saw Dad glowering down at us. What little fear space I had left in my small body immediately got filled up.

But if danger lurked in that canyon, so too did a magnetic attraction, a calling strong enough to drive two usually obedient boys across the threshold of direct disobedience, a singing siren that promised us more than a pretty song and a dashing on the rocks. It promised a way of life. It promised to seep inside our veins and to become a part of our marrow, raising up for us the sounds of its broken stream and the sighs of its leaning trees long after we had quit its ragged paths and settled in faraway cities. It was the call of the land we heard that day.

Topographically, there is little particularly unique or arresting about the ravine that bumped up against what was soon to be our property line in Sagamore Hills, Ohio. It is but one of a half dozen miniature canyons which thread their tedious ways to the slow flowing waters of the Cuyahoga River at the bottom of the valley, perhaps not even a half mile in a straight line. It begins as little more than a low-lying natural ditch, once fed by a small spring, now dried out, which drains a few gentle slopes in that nook of northern Summit County. For those few hundred feet it was known as "Jensiks' Creek."   At about the place where our oddly shaped property came to a triangular point Jensiks' Creek runs over a small waterfall of perhaps 20 or 30 feet, easily the most interesting feature of the area's physical landscape and the one that earned our blandly generic name," the falls."   Even here it is insignificant compared to its neighboring ravine a quarter of a mile to the south cut by historic Brandywine Creek and boasting magnificent

Brandywine Falls. But Brandywine Creek and Falls belonged to
people like David Hudson, who paddled his way to his more
famous township nearly two centuries ago, or, more recently, to the
Cuyahoga Valley National Park. The falls, lower casing and all,
belonged to us.

"Belong" is a funny word, especially as it relates to land. In
this country our use of it has always bordered on the laughable, if
not the absurd. We shuffle a few pieces of paper among three or
four people in some distant bank office, then proclaim to the world
that we "own" a piece of land an acre across, several thousand miles
deep, and four billion years old. I once heard a Native American try
to explain how foreign such a concept was to the indigenous folks
of North America. She said, *You white people talk about how easy it
was to cheat an Indian out of his land. But to that Indian selling a piece of
land made no more sense than selling a piece of the sky. It never occurred
to him that it was his to sell. He figured he had cheated you out of those
beads and trinkets.*

Our ownership of the falls and that ravine was an Indian
ownership. If, as rarely happened, a nervous neighbor shouted us
away from it we would respond to our acknowledgment of adult
authority and leave it fast enough. But it never occurred to us not to
come back. It was either there for everybody or nobody, and the
latter alternative seemed an absurd waste. Had my parents persisted in their early command to stay away from it, we would have
had to disobey again, sooner or later.

Every kid has some piece of the world, no matter how
small, which is his or her special place. It is usually an obscure bit
of nothingness which the adult world doesn't want--probably
because they can't make any money off of it—a rotted stump, a
basement corner, an abandoned car. The only two prerequisites for
such a special place are that no one else knows of it (or at least has
no interest in it) and that it unfailingly provides a dusting of magical charm. Our special place sprawled out over 2,000 acres and
probably had not changed appreciably in the 20,000 years since the
last piece of the Wisconsin Glacier had died a warm, watery death
prostrated among its ancient hummocks. "The woods" offered us a

child's infinity of time and space and salamanders. No matter how hard we pounded on her earthen shoulders, or screamed into her earlike caves, or pulled her grapevine hair that tumbled carelessly from her treetops, she only smiled sleepily and went about her ancient business.

Several years ago my eight-year old heart drove my middle-aged body down the length of that ravine to its insignificant spillage into the Cuyahoga at the bottom of Red Lock Hill. I was slightly shocked to realize that, as a kid, I had never made the trip all the way down the valley. I guessed that, in part, this was because of the impatient curiosity of youth that caused us to quickly lose interest in one creek bottom and cut cross-country in pursuit of other parallel ravines. But the better reason was that these woods and these ravines, not the Cuyahoga River, was our destination in those days. It was an end in itself. We had no reason to seek the creek's terminus. It was mid-January, and I found our old special place in splendid form. A dusting of snow enhanced the magic, draping my childhood images with protective cobwebs, as if untouched since I had left them a third of a century before. The creek, broken by millions of rocks and weaving its torturous way downward with the patience born of an infinite sense of time, was about 80% frozen over. I played a continuous game with the thin panes of ice, trying to jump off of the groaning, cracking surfaces before they opened under me, enticed by the chance prospect that water depth beneath the ice could either be two inches or two feet. As always, the creek didn't mind. It would have ample time to heal the cracks or, upon a different whim, melt them away altogether. At intervals the stream broke into open water, each spot adding a part to the splashing chorus.

In spite of Nature's sometimes sloppy housekeeping I was amazed at how clearly this old "house" told its story, to which I had been oblivious as a kid. The Berea Sandstone outcroppings stacked outward over the creek below, with the longest thrusts of the plates at the top and the shorter ones cutting back beneath them, in opposing image to the shape of the ravine, itself. The softer beds of shales, however, mirrored the slopes of the ravine walls, cutting back as they rose to create angles of less than ninety degree. Both of these rock formations were obediently following geological house rules, with the tremendously resistant sandstone almost impervious to the slashing water, while the shale below eroded quickly. Everything reflected the mansion's multi-million year old blueprint. Not so with the furniture. The snapping sandstones and sliding shales mixed with fallen trees to create a veritable junkyard at the creek bottom. But there was no sense of embarrassment about all of this. With little more than a shrug the ravine continued on its way, feeling no need to tell the perplexed observer that housekeeping is not its main job.

The trek was surprisingly short, taking less than an hour to reach the Cuyahoga below, near the National Park headquarters for the Cuyahoga Valley National Recreation Area. I was disappointed to see that the creek did not make a direct run for the river once it hit the valley floor, but rather was routed through a culvert under Highland Road and thence to its final destination just beyond the roadway leading to the old Jaite paper mill. I winced when I saw the final ignominy, a concrete ditch which carried these sacred waters of Jensiks' Creek and the falls to their tiny mouth, as if the old lady hadn't been quite able to make it on her own and needed the strong arm of the rest home attendant to complete her trip to the place where she could expel her waste waters.

But then, just where the stream made its ancient contribution to the Cuyahoga, I was rewarded by a wonderful sight—subtly lost or entirely unspectacular to any other eyes, but beautiful to mine. About six feet before the concrete ditch ended at the river's shore there began an escalating build-up of mud-silt that grew to several inches deep at the point where the creek and river waters first mingle. The concrete was totally obliterated, defeated, for those last few feet as the stream matter-of-factly reenacted a modest exercise it had been performing millions of years. There were bits of our back yard in that silt, and the creek was depositing them here at this train station on the Cuyahoga as faithfully as it had done since a time before there were people to notice it.

I frowned at the audacity of the boringly symmetrical

concrete ditch, then smiled as I looked at the primeval ooze which was calmly remaking the creek bed, even for a few inches. Our special place was still winning the war against human ownership, human encroachment.

The land still belonged to no one. And everyone.

The Latest News

Edward Beatty

Near the end of "the news at ten from around
our world" (terror alert, refugees stopped
at border, rehabbed celebrity with book
to sell) there's scraping, like fingernails
trying to tear through wood.

I turn off the radio, open kitchen door, enter
the garage, this winter night so like a cave.
Before I refill Lucy's bowl I stoop
as she stretches, rub her frail neck.

A whistle, like blown sand wearing stone.
Her breath? Mine? Or snow covering,
maybe closing, all roads?

New Year's Eve 2003

Edward Beatty

A half-frosted window riddled with starlight
and beyond, below a mock cedar chalet
mounted on an iced pole, two eyes

detect mine: a possum feeding on
spilled birdseed. No candles, no wine,
no laughter, and, too, no bullets or dynamite.

Standing Between War and Me, an Amaryllis

Pit Menousek Pinegar

My three dollar after Christmas amaryllis
finished its spectacular, eight-trumpet display
in February, was forgotten, shriveled,
dark, tucked in among aloe, fern,
dormant orchids. In March a rogue stalk
leaped up, then budded, then bloomed

on the day the first bombs exploded
in Baghdad. I, at my computer,
at six o'clock, the amaryllis at ten,
the TV at twelve, so that every glance
at the screen was a mind sweep over
the amaryllis—beauty to bombs,

blood red to blood, triumphant unexpected
flowering to those cut down out of season.
I can't bear the juxtaposition of blooming
and death. I move the plant,
but it can't stand on its own, needs
the support of the others to remain upright.

I came in last night. The blooming
was over—blood red had turned to
dry-blood-black, its passing
nearly complete in one day. Yesterday,
seven women and children were blown
to bits by U.S. Marines at a checkpoint.

What beauty, what hope will stand
between six o'clock and midnight now?
What living thing would dare to thrive?

In Memoriam

Robens Napolitan

It's a salmon memory, familiar to all
whose pasts rushed with the Columbia
over Celilo Falls before the big dam was built.

The thick, silver bodies jumped high,
backs humped like camels in a final effort
to honor the call of their far-off-birth.

The females rested then, before death,
in the shallows of their home creek,
to spawn eggs in the slate-colored gravel.

The wash of clear water was gentle where they
floated, belly up, ghosts from another time
who swim into our dreams at night.

An Old Turtle Knows Fear on the River

Samuel Fate Longmire

Alone and aged,
in a murky backwater slough of the mighty Ohio,
an old turtle knows fear on the River –

the death in its hidden currents,
where carcasses become snagged in sycamore roots
and sinewy, bony animal flesh bobs and twists until it is grey
and then white and then grey again,
and the hair has been swept from the skin –

the hopeless, slow tail-flopping
of half-dead catfish and carp
stranded in corn fields when the muddy floods recede –

the dark steel-shot horror of solitary geese
with jagged bone-ends protruding through matted feathers,
wounded by hunters and shitting puddles of green liquid,
slowly dying of infection and starvation on the sandy bank.

Peace

Michael Estabrook

soft sounds
of the stream
from back beyond
the trees seeping
in through
open windows
at night beneath
simmering
summer stars

If I Were A Tree

Aida K. Press

I would dress you
in golden leaves
and orange and red
to light up the
dying days
of the sun.

I would keep the sun
from burning
your beautiful face.

I would talk to the birds
that make nests on
my branches
and warn the squirrels
not to get too close.

I would gather your children
in my arms
and listen to their stories
and feed them ripe cherries

and send them home to you
before dark
before coyotes
could drag them away.

Firebrand

Carol Pearce Bjorlie

How blinding the brush fire,
each spark a potential threat.

I circle the heat, dodge smoke drafts,
jump at wood pop and branch split.
After the conflagration, I pull a stump close.

The sound of fire's a savage thing
until a burned trunk shifts
and gives up in a slump of embers.

At the fire's start
I never thought
which branch would be the final ember.

I want to burn like this:
a red-hot hope
in the dark.

Reminder

Richard Baldasty

It's OK
to take this page
tear it out or rip its corner
turn it to your employment
a place to jot a number
remember a title
prompt yourself to stop for bread
on the way home.

You might snip less than words
maybe only letters to print a note
which won't betray your handwriting:
please love me as I do you—or—
this is a stickup give me the money.

Fold once, twice, cut a snowflake.
Fold accordion style, a fan.

Make an airplane
a collage
a temporary shoe pad
a dozen thin strips to mark places
in a favorite novel: don't forget
Camus' old man whose world is bits
of paper he drifts upon cats
beneath his balcony.

But it's up to you
anything you choose
even if you just leave it
at least for now as is
a reminder use rearranges
and we in our time will serve
through many changes.

Out of Line

CONTRIBUTORS

Carol Alena Aronoff, Ph.D., psychologist and writer, taught Eastern spirituality and healing practices at San Francisco State. She co-authored *Practical Buddhism: The Kagyu Path* and published *Compassionate Healing: Eastern Perspectives.* Her poems have appeared in *Comstock Review, Poetica*, and *Theater of the Mind*, among others. She is a current Pushcart Prize nominee.

Barry Ballard has most recently placed his poetry in *The Evansville Review, Blue Mesa, Louisiana Literature*, and *The Florida Review.* His most recent collections are *First Probe to Antarctica* (Bright Hill Press Award for 2001) and *Plowing to the End of the Road* (Finishing Line Press Award for 2002 and nominated for the Pushcart Prize).

Mary Barrett, a public school teacher in Berkeley, is a free lance writer. She writes articles for the *Berkeley Daily Planet* and has published autobiographical pieces. Her poems have won local awards and have been published in several literary journals.

In 2005 **Edward Beatty** had poems appear in *Fulcrum, Poetry East, Cider Press Review, Karamu, Willow Review, Crab Creek Review,* and others. After receiving an MA in American and British Literature from the University of Wisconsin he taught literature and philosophy until he retired early to concentrate on writing.

Brad Bennett is a third grade teacher in Concord, Massachusetts. His poems have appeared in several magazines and journals, including *Out of Line*. He was a major contributor to *Protest, Power, and Change: An Encyclopedia of Nonviolent Action from ACT-UP to Women's Suffrage*, edited by Roger S. Powers and William B. Vogele, 1997.

Carol Bergman, who teaches nonficiton writing at NYU, is a journalist. Her feature articles and essays have appeared in *The New York Times, Newsday,* and others. She has written two film biographies (Mae West, Sidney Poitier), and her creative non-fiction and literary fiction has appeared in numerous literary journals. She was nominated for the 1999 Pushcart Prize in nonfiction.

Lisa Bernardini has a poem, "Waiting for Dark," accepted for publication in the upcoming *Hurricane Anthology: In Our Own Voices.* She has been a featured reader at Poetry Upwellings and has the highest haiku scores in Orlando Slam History.

Carol Pearce Bjorlie is adjunct professor of music at the University of Wisconsin, River Falls, and poetry/creative process teacher at the Loft Literary Center in Minneapolis. Her poems appear in *Southern Poetry Review, Great River Review,* and *St. Andrews Review,* among others.

Louise A. Blum, Associate Professor of English at Mansfield University in Pennsylvania, is the author of, *Amnesty,* a novel, and *You're Not From Around Here, Are You? A Lesbian in Small-town America.* Her work has appeared in numerous anthologies, literary magazines, and professional journals. She lives in Corning, New York with her partner, Connie Sullivan-Blum and their daughter Zoe, 8.

Alice Bolstridge has publications of fiction, poetry, and creative nonfiction in a wide variety of literary magazines and anthologies: *Cimarron Review* (1985 winner Oklahoma State Poetry and Fiction Awards); *Licking River Review* (1991 Best of Issue Poetry Prize); *Passager* (1995 *Passager Poet* Award); *Out of Line (2005)* and others.

Sandra Cookson is a member of the English faculty at Canisius College in Buffalo, New York. She teaches creative writing and literature courses and is currently chair of the English department. Her poems have appeared in a number of literary magazines.

Robert Cooperman's two latest collections, *A Killing Fever* (Ghost Road Press) and *The Long Black Veil* (Higganum Hill Books) are forthcoming in 2006. *In the Colorado Gold Fever Mountains* (Western Reflections) won the Colorado Book Award in 2000. *A Tale of the Grateful Dead* came out in 2004 from Main Street Rag Press.

Louie Crew is the author of more than 1,650 publications and an emeritus professor of English at Rutgers University. He serves on the Executive Council (Board of Governors) of the Episcopal Church and is the founder of Integrity, the gay and lesbian ministry of Episcopalians. He and Ernest Clay married in 1974 and live in East Orange, N.J.

Kelly Cunnane, a writing instructor at University of Maine at Machias, lives on an island down east with her children, writing children's books and creative nonfiction. Her book, *For You Are a Kenyan Child*, with Atheneum, will be out spring, 2005, and her creative nonfiction pieces can be found in *The Christian Science Monitor* and in various magazines and anthologies, such as the recent *Maine Voices*.

Anne Da Vigo is an award-winning journalist and public relations professional. She co-authored *Coffee and Ink: How a Writers Group Can Nourish Your Creativity (Quill Driver Press, 2004)*. She reads an original story on a recently-released CD, *Light of Day*.

Annie Dawid's last book is *Lily in the Desert: Stories* (Carnegie Mellon Univ. Press). *In Dostoyevsky's Atmosphere* is part of *And Darkness Was Under His Feet*, other sections of which are appearing in *Poetica, Paper Street,* and online at writersite.com, where "Calisthenics: 1950 Bucharest" won second prize in the Arthur Edelstein fiction contest.

Orman Day's essays, short stories, and poetry have appeared in such journals as *Creative Nonfiction, Portland Review, Ascent, Red Cedar Review,* and *Poetry Motel.* He is currently writing a book about his backpacking experiences in 90 countries and the 50 states.

Diane E. Dees is a writer and psychotherapist in Louisiana. Two of her poems were recently read on the NPR program, "Theme and Variations," and more are scheduled to be read on Martha Stewart Living's "The Naturalist Datebook" on the Sirius Network.

Kirsten Dierking is the author of *One Red Eye* (Holy Cow! Press, 2001) a book of poetry about sexual assault. She received a poetry fellowship from the Minnesota State Arts Board, a Career Initiative Grant from the Loft Literary Center, and a master's degree in creative writing from Hamline University.

Louise Domaratius is a native of New Jersey residing in France, where she has taught English in the public schools and French to asylum-seekers. She is the author of two novels, *Gadji* and *Writing the Book of Ester*, essays, book reviews, and numerous short stories.

Juditha Dowd has appeared in *The Florida Review, Earth's Daughters, Up and Under*, and *Journal of New Jersey Poets*, among others.

Michael Estabrook is a medievalist disappointed (though reconciled) with the modern world, particularly with the materialism and mercantilism bludgeoning life, smashing our brains into the ground, our hearts into dust. He's still hoping to find a true and meaningful "cause" in life.

Sandy Feinstein spent 1998-1999 as a Fulbright Scholar in Syria. She has published poems about her experiences in Syria and Lebanon in *Princeton Arts Review, Facture*, and *Revista Atenea*, among others. She teaches English at Penn State Berks College.

Diana Fu has fiction in *The Claremont Review* and poetry in *Artword Quarterly* and *Poetry Motel*. She has collaborated with several translators and a journalist in Beijing on an English translation of a modern Chinese novel, *Telling the Premier the Truth*.

224

James Gage is a freelance writer and editor whose work has appeared or is forthcoming in *The Powhatan Review, The Iconoclast, Northern New England Review, Vermont Review,* and other publications.

Laura Gibson lives just outside of Philadelphia. When she's not teaching high school English, she hikes, rides her mountain bike, chats with her kids about what is true and good in the world, and writes— mostly fiction, but some poetry and nonfiction, too.

John Grey is an Australian born poet, playwright, and musician. His latest chapbook is *The Secret Address* from Snark Publishing. Recently his work has appeared in *Mobius, South Carolina Review,* and *The Malahat Review.*

Gregory Gilbert Gumbs grew up on the French/Dutch Caribbean Island of St. Martin/St. Maarten, and studied at the University of Utrecht, before coming to the U.S. He has published poems in poetry magazines and in anthologies in the Netherlands, the United States, India, Japan, France, the U.K., Australia, New Zealand and the Caribbean.

Merna Ann Hecht, storyteller, poet, arts and literacy educator, has been teaching creative writing and storytelling since 1978. She is the 1999 recipient of a National Storytelling Network Community Service award for her work as a storyteller and poet with at-risk and adjudicated youth. In 2002 she was awarded a Fishtrap Writers Institute Fellowship for poetry.

Elizabeth Ann James (Liz) in the last few years has won honors from The Akron Art Museum, The Dublin Arts Council, *The Atlanta Review, The Potomac Review,* and *Flashpoint.* Her poems have been published in over forty journals

Jerry Judge lives in Cincinnati with his wife and two sons and works as a social worker for Big Brothers Big Sisters. He has published two chapbooks: *No Forwarding Address* and *Father's Instinct* and poems in over thirty journals and magazines.

Jeffrey J. Knowles was for 30 years Director of the Statistical Analysis Center in the Ohio Office of Criminal Justice Services. He published *Integrity with Two Eyes: An Insider's Slant on the Moral Climate of Government* (University Press, 1999). He is also the author of religious publications including *What of the Night?* (Herald Press, 1992).

Ruth Anne Latta was one of eight co-winners of the City of Ottawa annual short story contest. Her most recent stories appear in *QFM: Quality Fiction for Women* (Reading, England) and *Green's Magazine* (Regina, SK). Her second collection of short stories, *Save the Last Dance for Me*, was published in 2002 by Poetica Press (Ottawa).

Bruce Lader has poems in *New York Quarterly, Poetry, Main Street Rag, Poet Lore, Sojourn, Powhatan Review, MARGIE,* and others. He is the founding director of Bridges Tutoring, Inc., a non-profit that enriches the learning of people from diverse socioeconomic and cultural backgrounds.

Julie Lechevsky is a massage therapist in Blacksburg, Virginia. In 2001 she won the Tennessee Chapbook Award for her collection, *Doll,* and in 2003 she won the Riverstone Poetry Chapbook Award for *I'm A Serious Something.* Her poems have appeared in *Hanging Loose, Pearl,* and *Southern Poetry Review,* among others.

Alexander Levering Kern is a poet and educator active in Quaker and peace and justice concerns. His work appears in anthologies and in *Georgetown Review, Caribbean Writer, Friends Journal,* and *Sacred Journey,* among others. He is editor of *Becoming Fire: Spiritual Writing from Rising Generations,* and directs the Faith Youth Institute at Andover Newton Theological School.

226

Elizabeth Levitski lives in the northwoods of Wisconsin with her husband. Her poems have appeared in many publications including *Atlanta Review, The Bitter Oleander,* and *Nimrod.*

Lyn Lifshin's book *Before It's Light* (Paterson Poetry Award, 2000) was published by Black Sparrow press, following their publication of *Cold Comfort* in 1997. *Another Woman Who Looks Like Me* (Black Sparrow-David Godine) is soon to appear. She has published more than 100 books of poetry and edited 4 anthologies of women's writing.

Joanne Lowery's poems have appeared in many literary magazines, including *Birmingham Poetry Review, Passages North, Atlanta Review,* and *Poetry East.* Her most recent collections are *Medusa's Darling* from March Street Press and *Seven Misters* from Pygmy Forest Press. She lives in Michigan.

Pam McAllister has written nonfiction books and edited anthologies on topics as diverse as the death penalty, Shakespeare, feminism, and nonviolence. Her most recent book is *Death Defying: Dismantling the Execution Machinery in 21st Century U.S.A.* Her poems have appeared in *Sinister Wisdom* and *Radical America,* and she has been a featured speaker at Brown, Johns Hopkins, and Princeton, among others.

James McLaughlin lives in Newton, Massachusetts, and attends Colby College in Waterville, Maine. His poems will soon appear in *Diner* and *Laundry Pen.*

Sally Allen McNall has lived, written, and taught in Kansas, New Zealand, Ohio, and California. Her chapbook, *How to Behave at the Zoo and Other Lessons,* was a winner of the 1997 State Street Press competition. Her first book, *Rescue,* won the Backwaters Press Prize, and was published in 2000.

John N. Miller taught for 35 years at Denison University, and he now finds himself living in "one of those elegant retirement ghettos, in Lexington, Virginia." He has published in many literary journals, including *Atlanta Review, Descant, North American Review, The Atlantic Monthly, Poetry, Prairie Schooner, Shenandoah,* and *The Georgia Review.*

Greg Moglia's work has appeared in *Paterson Literary Review, Lips, Birmingham Literary Review, Black Buzzard Review,* and two poetry anthologies, *Earth Shattering Poems* and *Roots and Flowers,* each edited by Liz Rosenberg. He is three times a winner of an Allan Ginsberg Poetry Award.

Elaine Morgan is a poet and freelance writer. Her works have appeared in *Midwest Poetry Review, Common Ground Review, New Press Literary Quarterly, The Aurora,* and *Museletter,* among others.

Wilda Morris is the coordinator of Shalom Education and the author of *Stop the Violence: Educating Ourselves to Protect Our Youth* (Judson Press). Her poetry has appeared in *Alive Now, Secret Place, Horizons, StreetWise,* and *Frogpond,* among others.

Cristina Perissinotto was born in Northern Italy; she is assistant professor of Italian Studies at the University of Ottawa. Her poetry has appeared in various magazines and anthologies, including the *Antigonish Review* and *The Lucid Stone.* She has published academic articles on Renaissance and contemporary literature.

Adrian Potter has won awards for his writing, including the 2003 Langston Hughes Poetry Contest and the December 2004 Point of Life Poetry Contest. He has been published in *Talking Stick, Loop, City Works, Deconstruction Quarterly,* and *The Rockford Review,* among others. He lives in Minneapolis.

Shirley Powers is the author of *With No Slow Dance* (Two Steps in Press). Her work has appeared in *Earth's Daughters, Iowa Woman, Wisconsin Review,* and *many* others. She won First Place 1995 Encore Poetry Magazine Contest, and was 2004 winner of City Reflections: San Francisco Library.

Aida K. Press is editor emerita of the *Radcliffe Quarterly.* She has studied with poets Ruth Whitman and Kinereth Gensler and is currently a student of Suzanne Berger. Her poems have been published in *Out of Line* and in the anthology, *Women Runners, Stories of Transformation.*

Diane Raptosh has published two books of poems: *Just West of Now* (Guernica, 1992) and *Labor Songs* (Guernica, 1999). Her work has appeared in *Terrain.org: A Journal of the Built and Natural Environments,* and *Kalliope,* among others. She holds the Eyck-Berringer Endowed Chair in the English Department at Albertson College of Idaho.

David Radavich's recent poetry collections are *By the Way (Buttonwood, 1998)* and *Greatest Hits* (Pudding House, 2000). His plays have been widely performed in the U.S. and Europe, including five productions Off-Off-Broadway. His recent project is a scholarly work entitled *The Midwestern Ground of American Drama.*

Tony Reevy is associate director for advancement of the Carolina Environmental Program at the University of North Carolina at Chapel Hill. His poetry has appeared in *Charlotte Poetry Review, Pembroke Magazine, Writer's Cramp,* and others. His poems also appear in anthologies, including *Poets for Peace: A Collection,* and his books include *Ghost Train!: American Railroad Ghost Legends.*

Kenneth Rehill provides behavioral health services to residents of remote villages in Alaska's northern interior. His poems have appeared in *Creosote, Poetic Voices, Timber Creek Review,* and others. His *Poems from the Gwitch'in Land* was released by the Indian Heritage Council.

John Roman, artist and writer, is an instructor at the Massachusetts College of Art in Boston. He was a victim of child abuse and is writing a book recounting his childhood trauma experiences as well as documenting his efforts to heal those early wounds. His story, *"Partners in Crime,"* is a chapter from that book.

Arthur Saltzman is a Professor of English at Missouri Southern State University and has written several books of criticism on contemporary American literature. In addition, he is the author of two essay collections: *Objects and Empathy,* which won the First Series Creative Nonfiction Award (Mid-List Press),and *Nearer* (Parlor Press).

Steven Schild teaches journalism and interdisciplinary studies at Saint Mary's University in Winona, Minnesota. His poems have appeared in the anthologies *Witness* (anti-war poems by Serengeti Press) and *33 Minnesota Poets* (Nodin Press). He has poems in a number of literary magazines, most recently *White Pelican Review* and *Elysian Fields Quarterly.*

Yvette A. Schnoeker-Shorb works as a mentor for Prescott College and as co-publisher of Native West Press. Her poetry has appeared in such journals as *Weber Studies: Voices and Viewpoints of the Contemporary West, The Midwest Quarterly, So to Speak: A Feminist Journal of Language and Art*, as well as in anthologies such as *The Blueline Anthology* and *New Century North American Poets.*

Nancy Scott is currently a VISTA volunteer working with homeless individuals and families. She is a repeat contributor to *Out of Line.* Her poetry has also appeared in *Witness, Journal of New Jersey Poets, Rattapallax, Slipstream,* and other literary journals.

John Simonds, a retired Honolulu newspaper editor and resident of Hawaii, has found writing verse is a useful and challenging way to revisit personal experience. His media career of 45 years included work with UPI in Columbus, Ohio, and its client newspapers throughout Ohio.

Arthur Slate has published poems in various literary journals, including *Poetry Motel, The Christian Science Monitor, The Old Red Kimono,* and *The Santa Barbara Review.*

J.D. Smith's second collection of poems, *Settling for Beauty,* (Cherry Grove Collections, 2005) is a Forbes Book Club selection. His essays have appeared in *Grist, Laurel Review,* and *Pleiades.* He lives and works in Washington, DC.

David Starkey teaches at Santa Barbara City College and is in the MFA program at Antioch University-Los Angeles. He is the author of *Poetry Writing: Theme and Variations* (NTC, 1999) and several collections: *Fear of Everything* (winner of Palanquin Press's Spring 2000 chapbook contest) and *David Starkey's Greatest Hits* (Pudding House, 2002).

Ann Struthers has published in *The North American Review, The American Scholar, Poetry, The Hudson Review,* and others. She has two collections and two chapbooks. She has written about her experiences living in Sri Lanka and in Syria where she taught at the University of Aleppo on a Fulbright Fellowship.

Elizabeth Swados has published three novels, two nonfiction books and a memoir. She has a children's book coming out with Scholastic and a book of humor and cartoons with Hyperion. Her poems have been published in several journals including *Barrow Street* and *Speakeasy.* She is an internationally known composer and playwright.

Christine Swanberg has published books of poetry, most recently *The Tenderness of Memory* (Plainview Press, 1995) and *The Red Lacquer Room* (Chiron Press, 2001). Her poems have appeared in numerous anthologies and literary journals, including *Beloit Poetry Journal* and *Amelia.*

Elizabeth Weir reviews Twin Cities' theater for Talkinbroadway.com. Her poetry has been published in *American Poetry Quarterly, Sidewalks,* and *ArtWord Quarterly,* the award-winning 2003 anthology, *Voices for the Land,* among others. Her poems will also appear in *Secondwind* and *Northstone Review.*

R. Yurman has published in many magazines and journals, including *Zone Three, Slipstream, The Ledge, New York Quarterly, The Berkeley Poetry Review,* and *The Beloit Poetry Journal.* His most recent chapbook, *Fascination Dolls,* was published in 2003 by Snark Publishing.

Allison Whittenberg holds a M.S. from the University of Wisconsin. She is the author of the novel *Sweet Thang* (Random House, 2006) and a collection of poetry, *The Bard of Philadelphia* (Rosewater Press, 2003). She is a native of Philadelphia.

Julie Herrick White has published *Friends from the Other Side* (chapbook, State Street Press), *Steubenville* (poem sequence, Pearl Editions), *Unfinished Business* (Nightshade Press), *Greatest Hits, 1981-2000* (Pudding House Publications), and *Uncle Gust and the Temple of Healing* (short fiction, Writers' Center Press of Indianapolis).

Morgan Grayce Willow's work in the translation of poetry from English to American Sign Language (ASL) & vice versa led to the publication of a guide for making literary events accessible to deaf audiences entitled, *Crossing That Bridge.* Other publications include a chapbook entitled *Spinnerets.*

Beadrin Youngdahl, a registered nurse and a member of the Minneapolis Writers Workshop, writes short fiction, essays and poetry. "*The Kerchief*" was written in response to a recent trip to Africa to learn more about the AIDS epidemic.

Out of Line